PIANO • VOCAL • GUITAR

FAVORITE
Christmas C

ISBN 0-634-01695-4

HAL•LEONARD®
CORPORATION
7777 W. BLUEMOUND RD. P.O. BOX 13819 MILWAUKEE, WI 53213

Visit Hal Leonard Online at
www.halleonard.com

CONTENTS

ALL MY HEART THIS NIGHT REJOICES

Words by PAULUS GERHARDT
and HORATIO PARKER
Translated by CATHERINE WINKWORTH

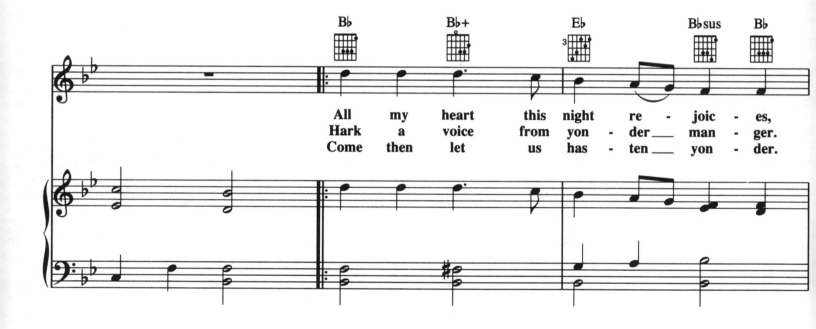

All my heart this night re - joic - es,
Hark a heart voice from yon - der __ man - ger.
Come then let us has - ten __ yon - der.

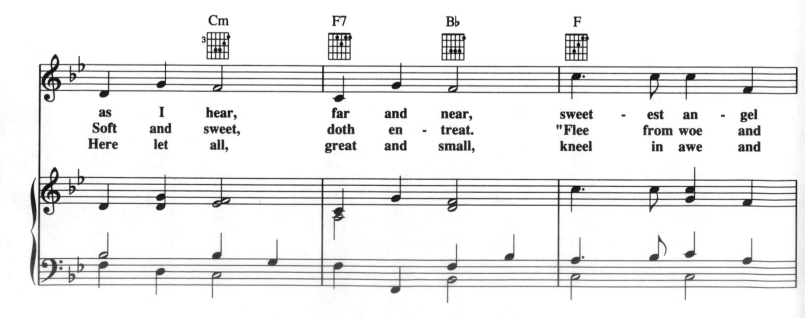

as I hear, far and near, sweet - est an - gel
Soft and sweet, doth en - treat. "Flee from woe and
Here let all, great and small, kneel in awe and

C7sus C7 F Cm

voic - es. "Christ is born," their
dan - ger. Breth - ren come from
won - der. Love Him who with

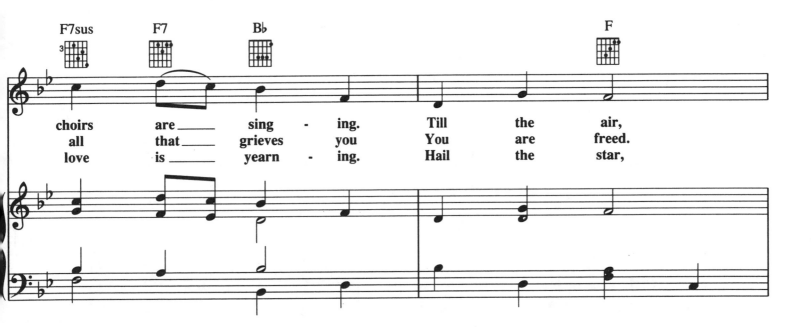

F7sus F7 Bb F

choirs are ___ sing - ing. Till the air,
all that ___ grieves you You are freed.
love is ___ yearn - ing. Hail the star,

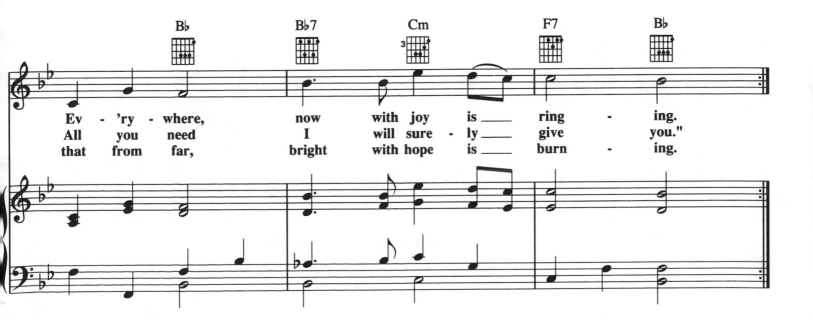

Bb Bb7 Cm F7 Bb

Ev - 'ry - where, now with joy is ___ ring - ing.
All you need I will sure - ly ___ give you."
that from far, bright with hope is ___ burn - ing.

ALL THROUGH THE NIGHT

Moderately

Traditional

Sleep, my Child, and peace at - tend Thee, All through the
While the moon her watch is keep - ing, All through the

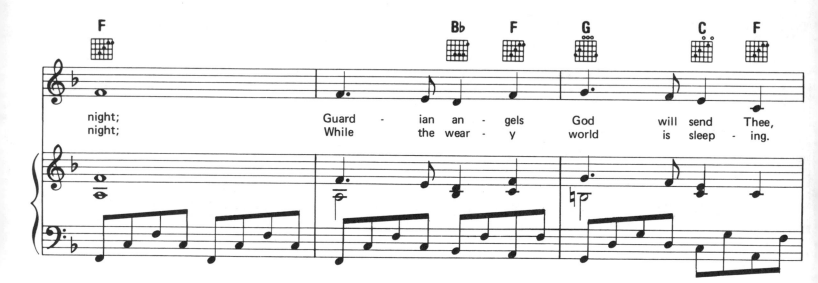

night;   Guard - ian an - gels God will send Thee,
night;   While the wear - y world is sleep - ing.

All through the night.   Soft the drow - sy
All through the night,   Through your dreams you're

ANGELS FROM HEAVEN

Hungarian

ANGELS FROM THE REALMS OF GLORY

Words by JAMES MONTGOMERY
Music by HENRY SMART

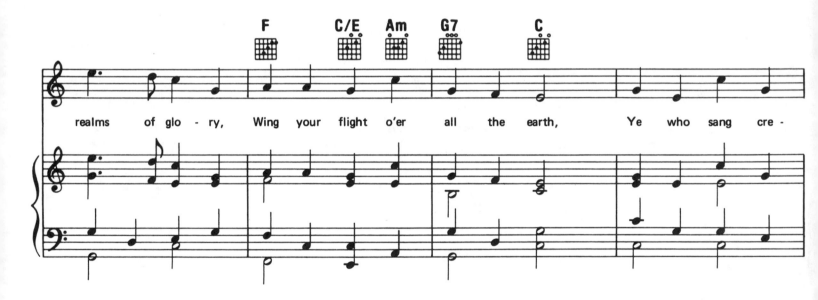

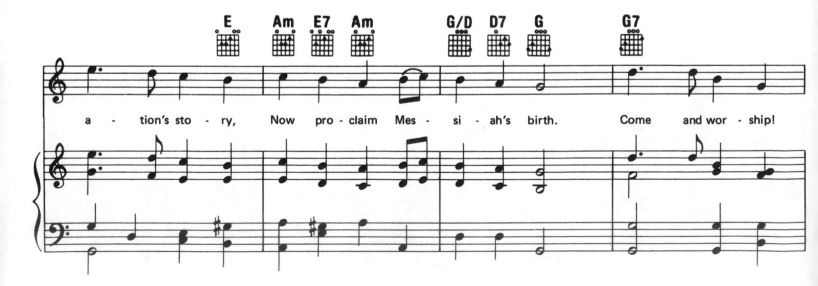

ANGELS WE HAVE HEARD ON HIGH

Moderately

French-English

An - gels we have heard on high Sweet - ly sing - ing

o'er the plains, And the moun - tains in re - ply

Ech - o - ing their joy - ous strains. Glo -

AS LATELY WE WATCHED

Austrian

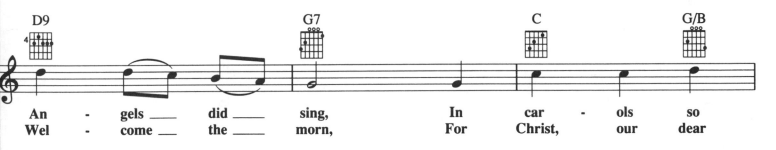

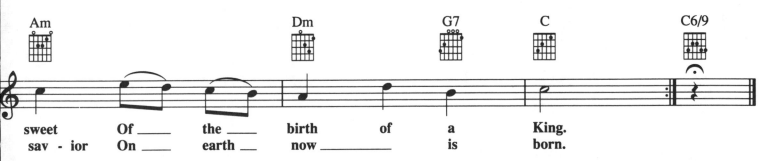

3. Then shepherds, be joyful,
   Salute your liege King;
   Let hills and dales ring
   To the song that ye sing:
   Blest be the hour,
   Welcome the morn,
   For Christ, our dear Saviour,
   On earth now is born.

AS WITH GLADNESS MEN OF OLD

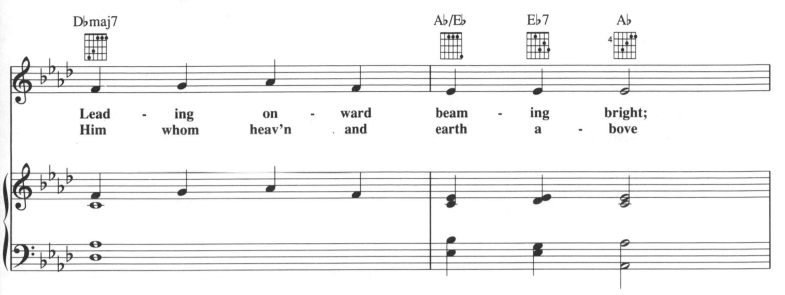

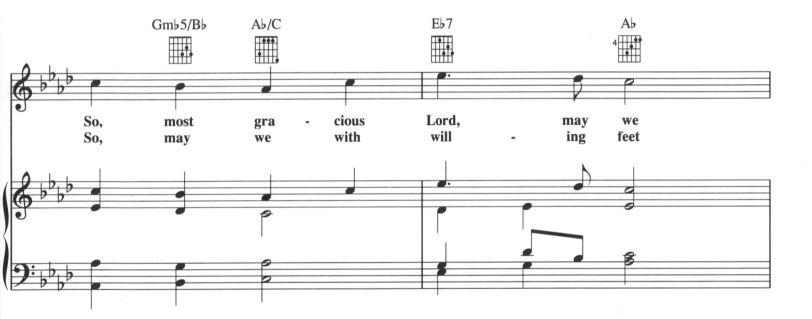

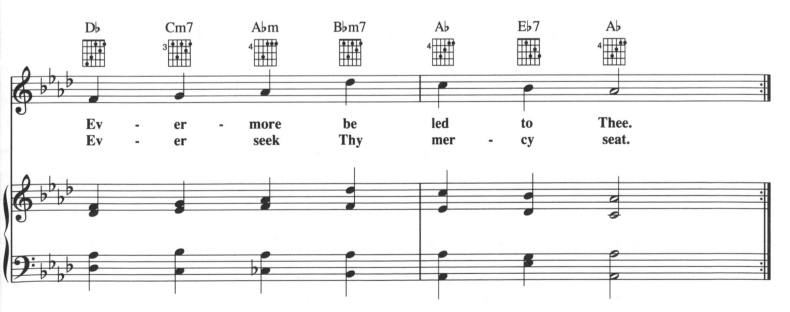

3. As they offered gifts most rare,
   So may we with holy joy,
   All our costliest treasures bring,
   At that manger rude and bare,
   Pure and free from sin's alloy,
   Christ, to Thee, our heav'nly King.

AT THE HOUR OF MIDNIGHT

Puerto Rican

La la la la la la la la la la la la la la la la la la

la la la la la la la la la la la la la la La

la. At the hour of mid - night,__ In the midst of win - ter,__
Heav-en's King e - ter - nal __ On the straw is ly - ing.__

3. Mary weeps in pity for suff'ring darling,
   Wishing for protection from the cold winds howling
   "Tend'rest little infant Savior, O my Jesus,
   All my love forever, sweetest Son so precious."

AWAY IN A MANGER

Words by MARTIN LUTHER
Music by JONATHAN E. SPILLMAN

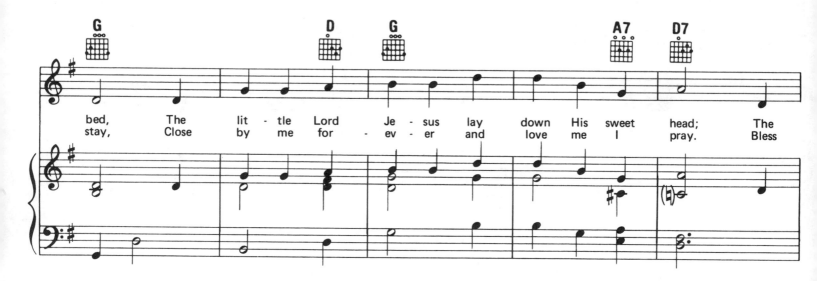

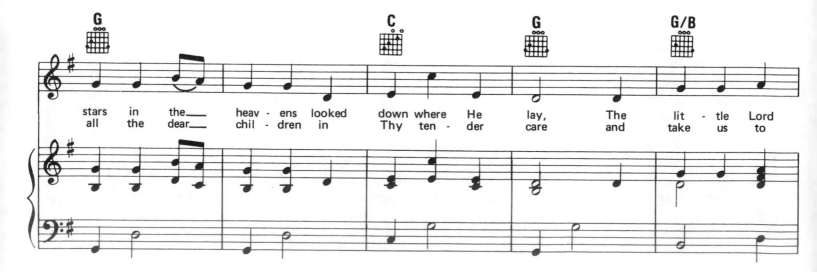

AWAY IN A MANGER

Words by MARTIN LUTHER
Music by CARL MUELLER

Sweetly

A -

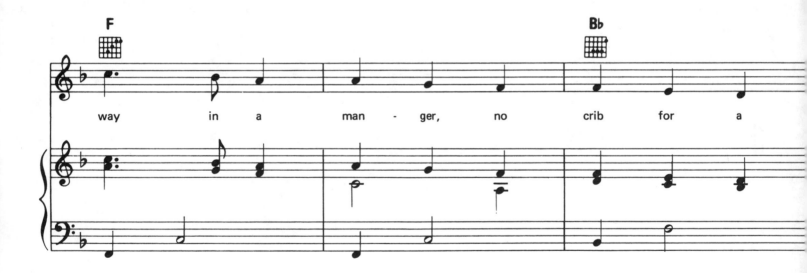

way in a man - ger, no crib for a

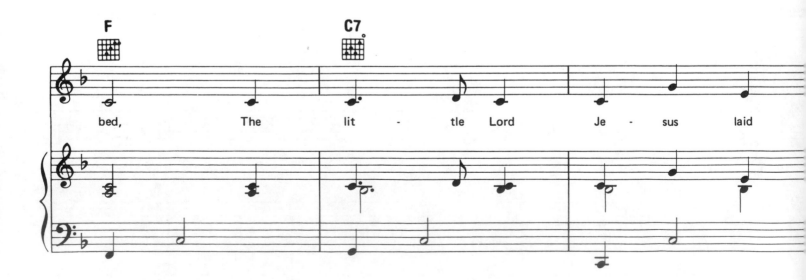

bed, The lit - tle Lord Je - sus laid

A BABE IS BORN IN BETHLEHEM

Words and Music by
LUDWIG LINDEMAN

3. The wise men came, led by the star;
   Gold, myrrh and incense, brought from afar.
   Hallelujah, Hallelujah.

4. On This most blessed Jubilee, blest Jubilee;
   All glory be, O god, to Thee.
   Hallelujah, Hallelujah

THE BABY IN THE CRADLE

Words and Music by
D.G. CORNER

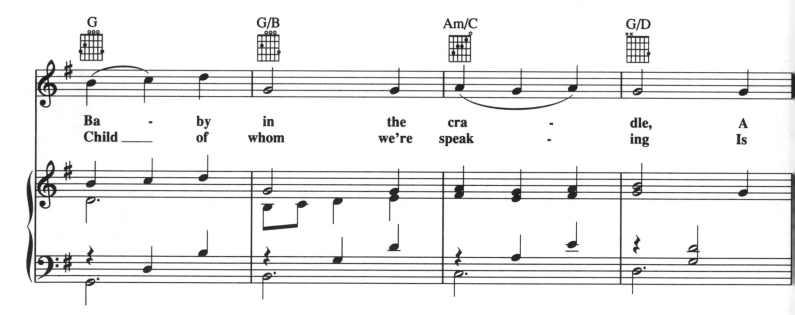

Ba - by in the cra - dle, A
Child ___ of in whom we're speak - ing Is

ti - ny Child ___ so bright; _____ He
Jes - us Christ, ___ the Lord; _____ He

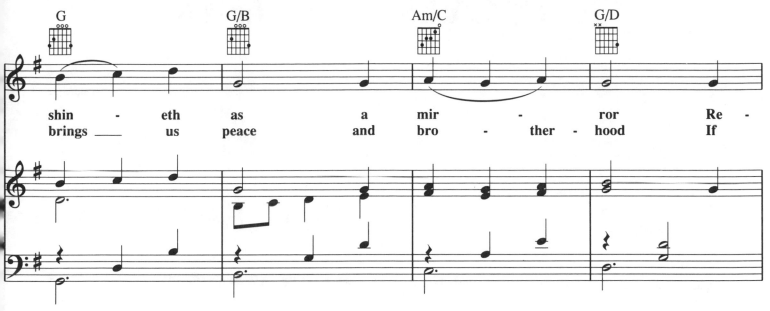

shin - eth as a mir - ror Re -
brings ___ us peace and bro - ther - hood If

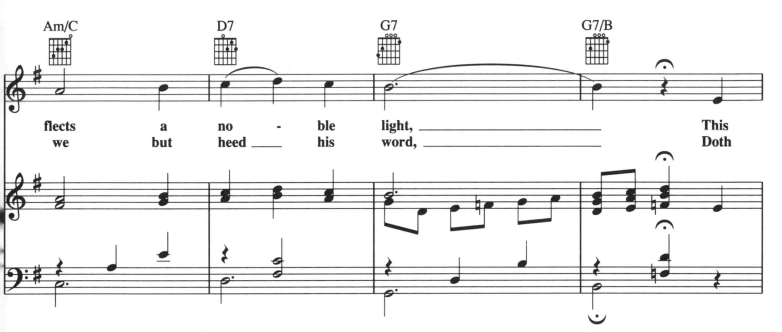

flects a no - ble light, _____ This
we but heed ___ his word, _____ Doth

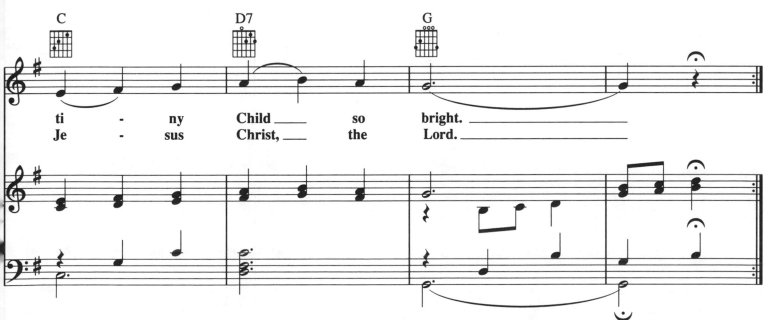

ti - ny Child ___ so bright. _____
Je - sus Christ, ___ the Lord. _____

3. And he who rocks the cradle
   Of this sweet Child so fine
   Must serve with joy and heartiness,
   Be humble and be kind,
   For Mary's Child so fine.

4. O Jesus, dearest Savior,
   Although Thou art so small,
   With Thy great love o'erflowing
   Come flooding through my soul,
   Thou lovely Babe so small.

BELLS OVER BETHLEHEM

Andalucian Carol

BESIDE THY CRADLE HERE I STAND

THE BOAR'S HEAD CAROL

English

A BOY IS BORN IN BETHLEHEM

Latin

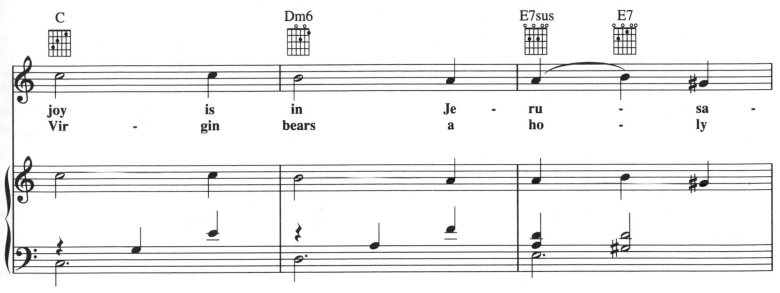

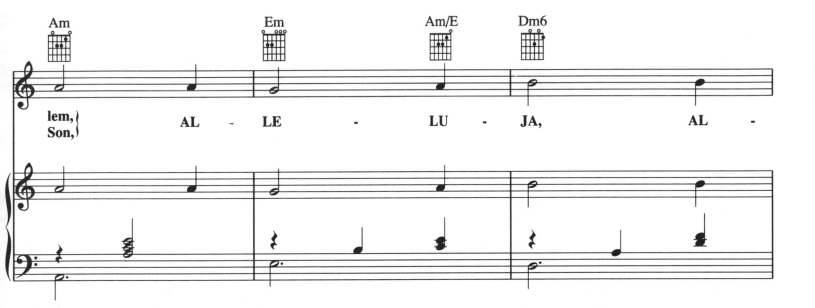

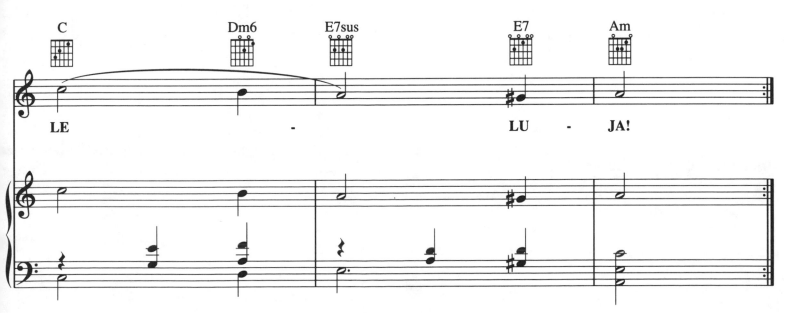

3. The wisest kings of Orient
   Gold, frankincense, and myrrh present.

4. Laud to the Holy Trinity,
   All thanks and praise to God most high.

BREAK FORTH, O BEAUTEOUS HEAVENLY LIGHT

Words and Music by JOHANN RIST
Adapted and harmonized by J.S. BACH
Translated by J. TROUTBECK

BRING A TORCH, JEANNETTE, ISABELLA

Provençal

Brightly

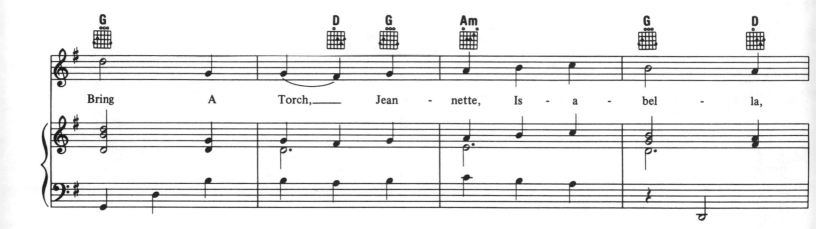

Bring A Torch,____ Jean - nette, Is - a - bel - la,

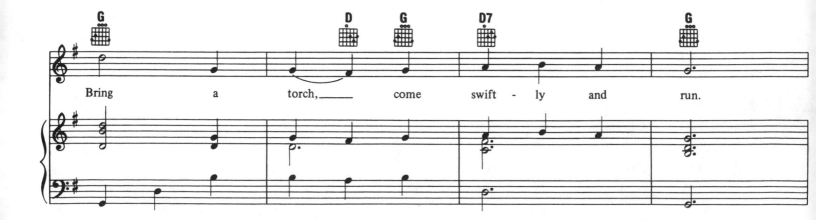

Bring a torch,____ come swift - ly and run.

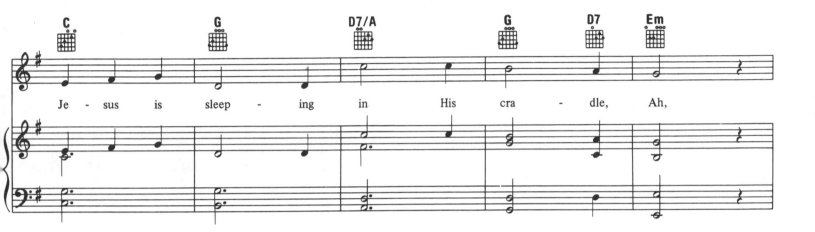

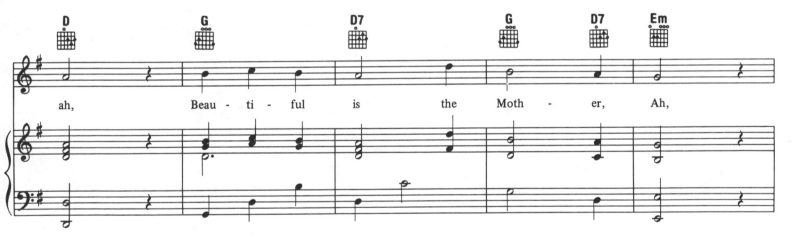

Hasten now, good folk of the village,
Hasten now, the Christ Child to see.
You will find him asleep in a manger,
Quietly come and whisper softly,
Hush, hush, Peacefully now He slumbers,
Hush, hush, Peacefully now He sleeps.

A CHILD IS BORN IN BETHLEHEM

Danish

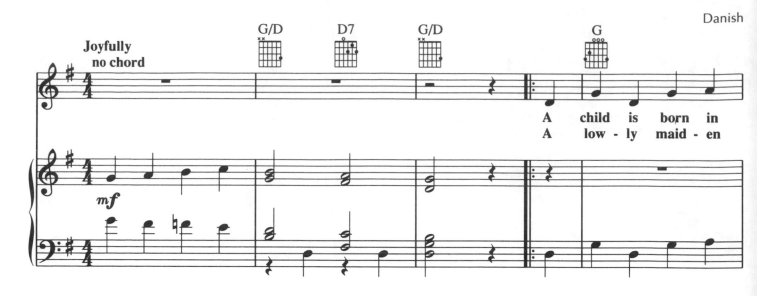

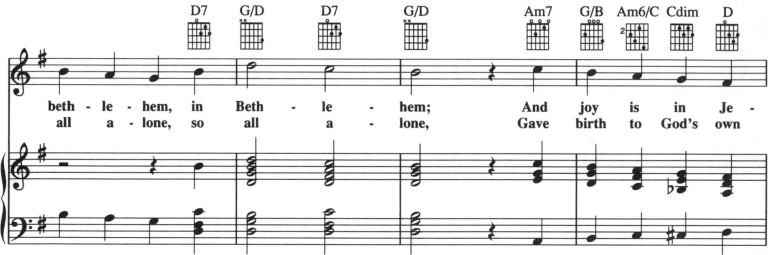

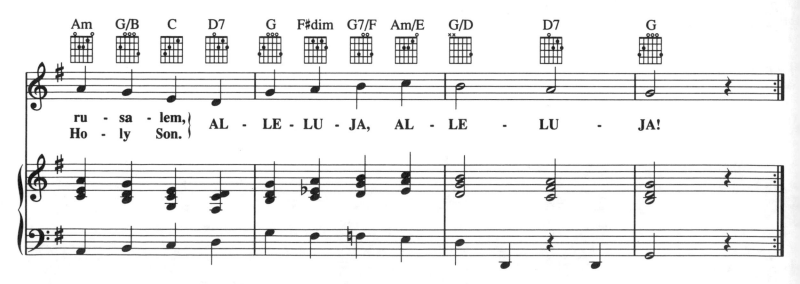

3. She chose a manger for His bed,
For Jesus' bed.
God's angels sang for joy o'erhead,
ALLELUJA, ALLELUJA!

4. Give thanks and praise eternally,
Eternally,
To God, the Holy Trinity.
ALLELUJA, ALLELUJA!

THE CHRISTMAS TREE WITH ITS CANDLES GLEAMING

German

3. For ev'ry heart, you offer blessing,
For ev'ry parent as well as child;
For young and old, your beacons beck'ning
Lead us to Jesus, sweet and mild.

CHILDREN GO WHERE I SEND THEE

One for the lit - tle bit - ty Ba - by,
Two for the Paul and Si - las,
Three for the He - brew chil - dren,

one for the lit - tle bit - ty Ba - by,
two for the Paul and Si - las,
three for the He - brew chil - dren,

Born born, _____ born in Beth - le - hem. _

Chil - dren _____

CHRIST IS BORN THIS EVENING

Polish

CHRIST WAS BORN ON CHRISTMAS DAY

German

CHRISTIANS, AWAKE! SALUTE THE HAPPY MORN

Words by JOHN BYROM
Music by J. WAINWRIGHT

COME ALL YE SHEPHERDS

Come, all ye shepherds such wonders enthrall Come where the young Child is laid in a stall. This day to us a Savior is given, Whom, God on high hath sent down from heaven Hallelujah!

COME, THOU LONG EXPECTED JESUS

Words by CHARLES WESLEY
Music by ROWLAND PRICHARD

Lyrics:

Come, Thou Long ___ ex-pect ___ -ed Je ___ -sus, Born to set Thy peo ___ -ple free.

Born Thy peo-ple to de-liv-er, Born a child and yet ___ a king.

THE COVENTRY CAROL

English, 16th Century

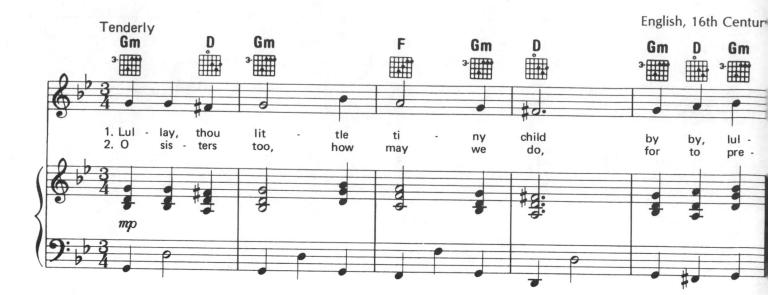

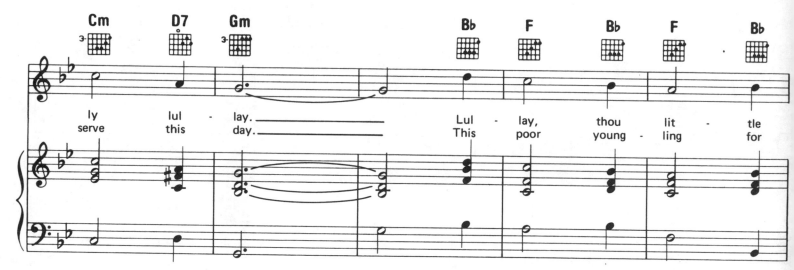

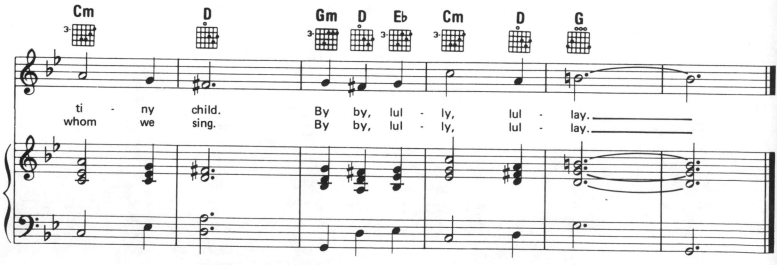

3. Herod the king,
   In his raging,
   Charged he hath this day.
   His men of might,
   In his own sight,
   All young children to slay.

4. That woe is me,
   Poor child for thee!
   And ever morn and day,
   For thy parting
   Neither say nor sing
   By by, lully lullay!

FROM HEAVEN ABOVE TO EARTH I COME

Words and Music by
MARTIN LUTHER

3. Glory to God in highest heav'n,
Who unto us his Son hath giv'n!
While angels sing with pious mirth,
A glad New Year to all the earth.

DECK THE HALL

Welsh

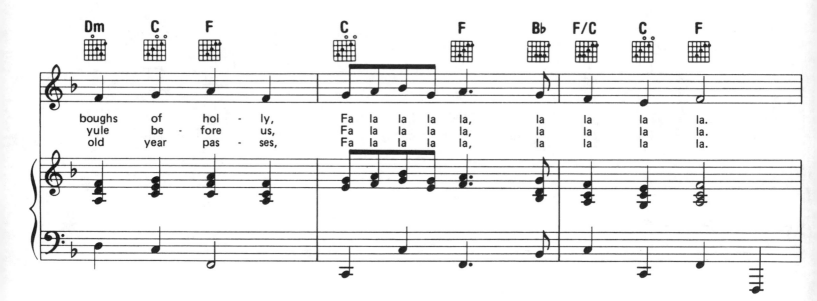

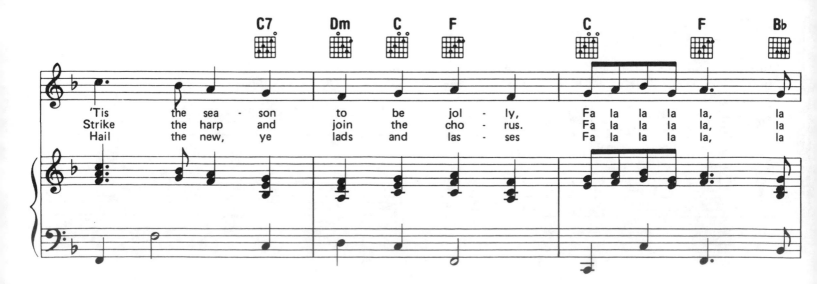

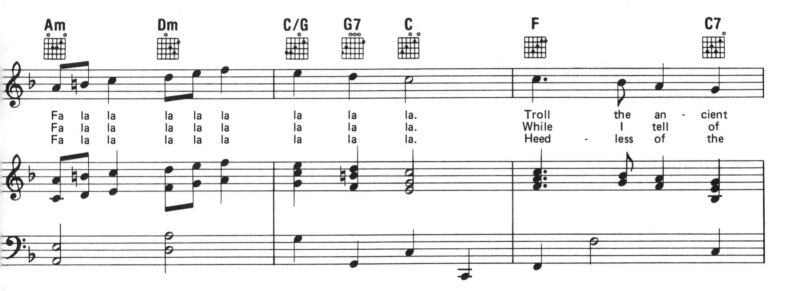

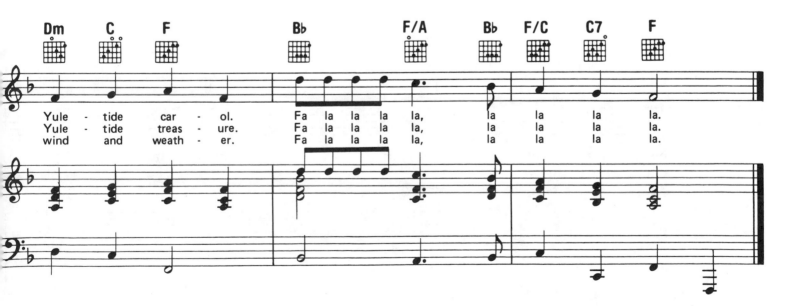

DING DONG! MERRILY ON HIGH

16th Century French Tune

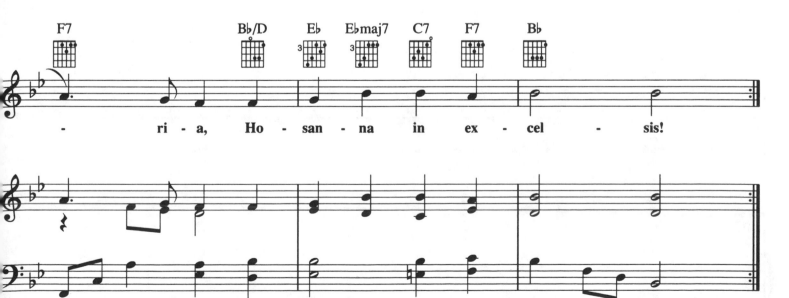

3. Pray you, dutifully prime your matin chime, ye ringers;
   May you beautiful rime your evetime song, ye singers.

THE FIRST NOEL

French-English

keep-ing their sheep, On a cold win-ter's night___ that was___ so

Refrain

deep. No - ël,___ No - ël, No - ël, No - ël,

Born is the King___ of Is - ra - el.

Additional Lyrics

2. They looked up and saw a star
   Shining in the East, beyond them far.
   And to the earth it gave great light
   And so it continued both day and night.
   Refrain

3. And by the light of that same star,
   Three wise men came from country far;
   To seek for a King was their intent,
   And to follow the star wherever it went.
   Refrain

4. This star drew nigh to the northwest,
   O'er Bethlehem it took its rest;
   And there it did both stop and stay,
   Right over the place where Jesus lay.
   Refrain

5. Then entered in those wise men three,
   Full reverently upon their knee;
   And offered there in His presence,
   Their gold, and myrrh, and frankincense.
   Refrain

THE FRIENDLY BEASTS

English

beasts a - round Him stood,

Je - sus our broth - er, kind and good.

Additional Lyrics

2. "I," said the donkey, shaggy and brown,
   "I carried His mother up hill and down;
   I carried her safely to Bethlehem town."
   "I," said the donkey, shaggy and brown.

3. "I," said the cow all white and red,
   "I gave Him my manger for His bed;
   I gave Him my hay to pillow His head."
   "I," said the cow all white and red.

4. "I," said the sheep with curly horn,
   "I gave Him my wool for His blanket warm;
   He wore my coat on Christmas morn."
   "I," said the sheep with curly horn.

5. "I," said the dove from the rafters high,
   "I cooed Him to sleep so He would not cry;
   We cooed Him to sleep, my mate and I."
   "I," said the dove from the rafters high.

6. Thus every beast by some good spell,
   In the stable dark was glad to tell
   Of the gift he gave Emanuel,
   The gift he gave Emanuel.

FROM THE EASTERN MOUNTAINS

Words by GODFREY THRING
Music by F.J. HAYDN

3. Thou who in a manger
   Once hast lowly lain,
   Who dost now in glory
   O'er all kingdoms reign,
   Gather in the heathen
   Who in lands afar
   Ne'er have seen the brightness
   Of Thy guiding star.

4. Gather in the outcasts,
   All who have astray,
   Throw Thy radiance o'er them,
   Guide them on their way,
   Those who never knew Thee,
   Those who have wandered far,
   Guide them by the brightness
   Of Thy guiding star.

5. Onward through the darkness
   Of the lonely night,
   Shining still before, them
   With Thy kindly light,
   Guide them, Jew and Gentile,
   Homeward from afar,
   Young and old together,
   By Thy guiding star.

FUM, FUM, FUM

Joyfully

Spanish

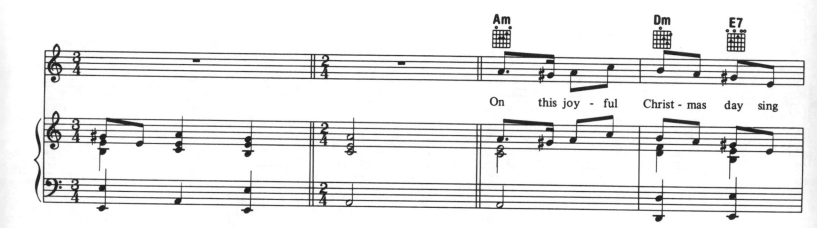

On this joy-ful Christ-mas day sing

Fum, Fum, Fum. On this joy-ful Christ-mas day sing

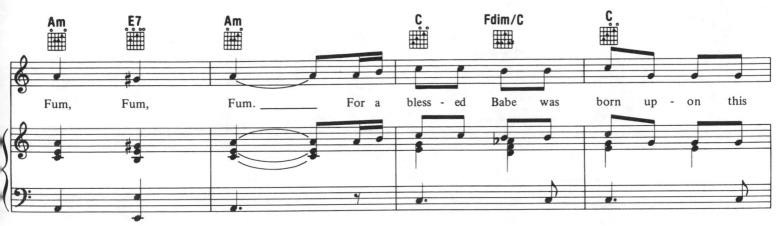

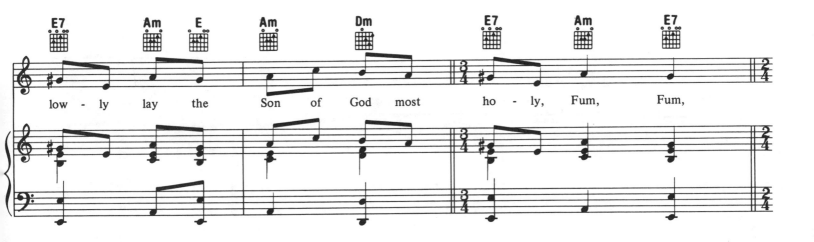

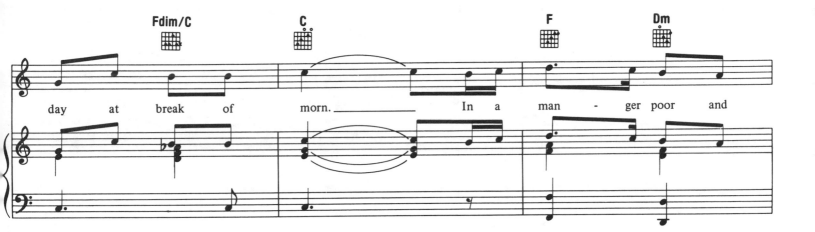

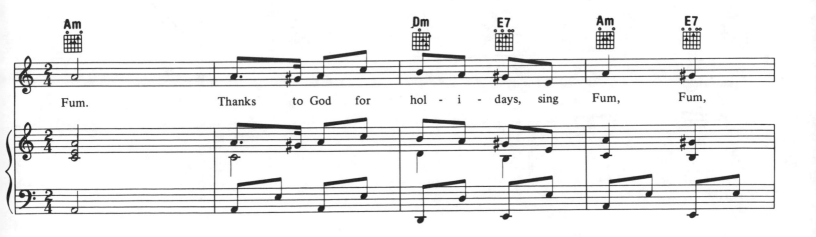

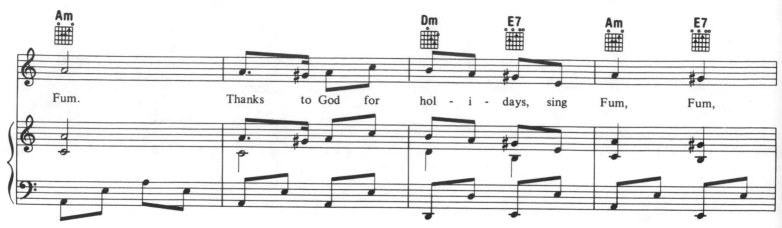

Fum. Thanks to God for hol - i - days, sing Fum, Fum,

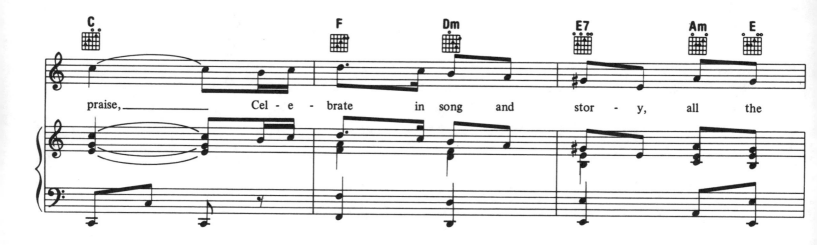

Fum. Now we___ all our voic - es raise, and sing a song of grate - ful

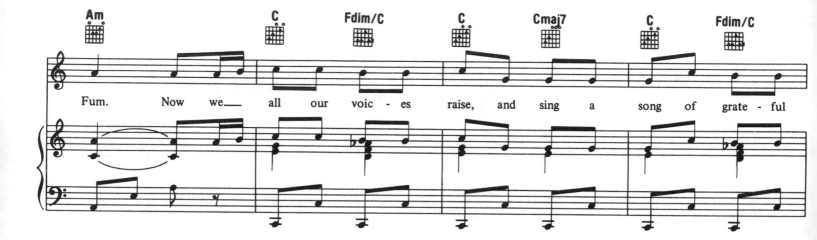

praise,_____ Cel - e - brate in song and stor - y, all the

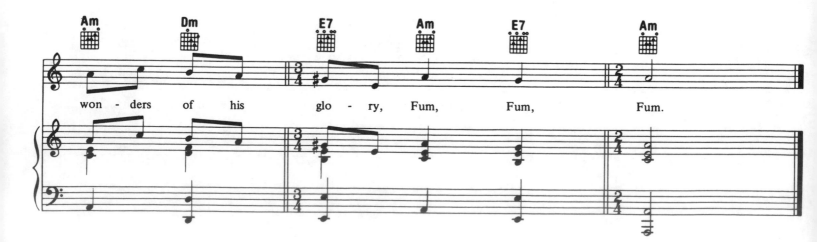

won - ders of his glo - ry, Fum, Fum, Fum.

GOOD CHRISTIAN MEN, REJOICE

German, 14th Century
Words translated by JOHN M. NEALE

GO TELL IT ON THE MOUNTAIN

African-American Spiritual

Lyrics: Go tell it on the moun - tain,

O - ver the hills and ev - 'ry - where; Go tell it on the

GOD REST YE MERRY, GENTLEMEN

3. From God our heav'nly Father,
A blessed Angel came;
And unto certain shepherds
Brought tidings of the same;
How that in bethlehem was born
The Son of God by Name.

GOOD KING WENCESLAS

Words by JOHN M. NEALE
Traditional Melody

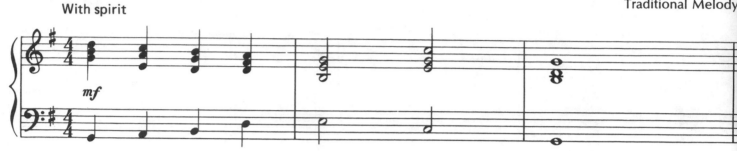

With spirit

mf

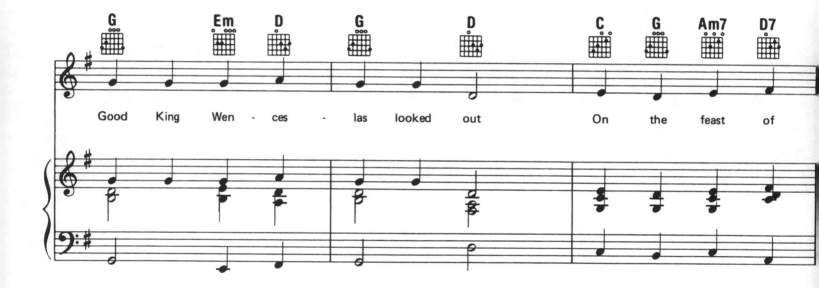

Good King Wen - ces - las looked out   On the feast of

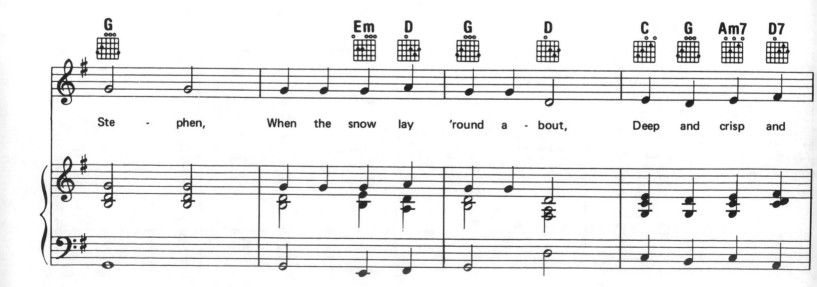

Ste - phen,   When the snow lay 'round a - bout,   Deep and crisp and

2.
"Hither page, and stand by me,
　If thou know'st it, telling,
Yonder peasant, who is he?
　Where and what his dwelling?"
"Sire, he lives a good league hence,
　Underneath the mountain;
Right against the forest fence,
　By Saint Agnes' fountain."

3.
"Bring me flesh, and bring me wine,
　Bring me pine-logs hither;
Thou and I will see him dine,
　When we bear them thither."
Page and monarch forth they went,
　Forth they went together;
Through the rude winds wild lament:
　And the bitter weather.

4.
"Sire, the night is darker now,
　And the wind blows stronger;
Fails my heart, I know not how,
　I can go not longer."
"Mark my footsteps, my good page,
　Tread thou in them boldly:
Thou shalt find the winter's rage
　Freeze thy blood less coldly."

5.
In his master's steps he trod,
　Where the snow lay dinted;
Heat was in the very sod
　Which the saint had printed.
Therefore, Christain men, be sure,
　Wealth or rank possessing,
Ye who now will bless the poor,
　Shall yourselves find blessing.

HALLELUJAH CHORUS

(From The "Messiah")

George Frideric Handel

HARK! THE HERALD ANGELS SING

Words by CHARLES WESLEY
Music by FELIX MENDELSSOHN-BARTHOLDY

Joyfully

Hark! The Her - ald An - gels Sing,_____
"Glo - ry to the new - born King! Peace on earth, and

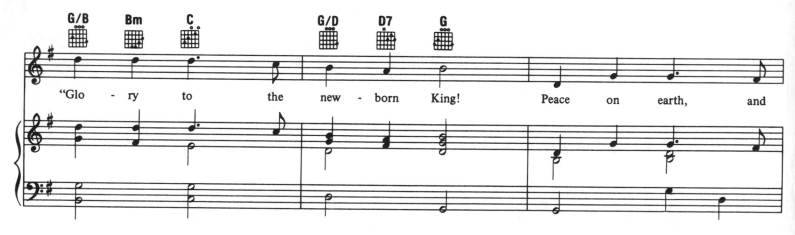

mer - cy mild,_____ God and sin - ners re - con - ciled."

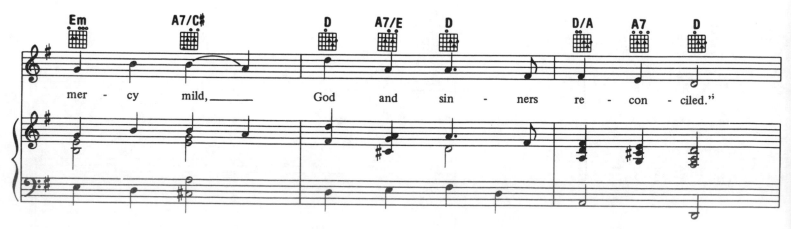

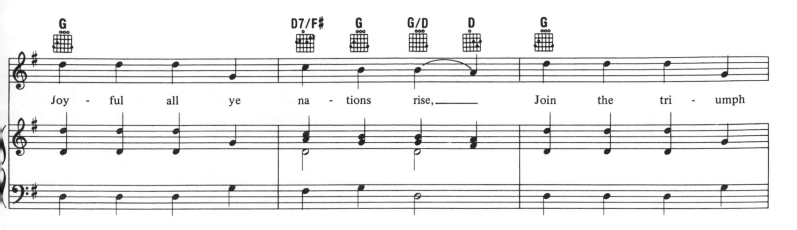

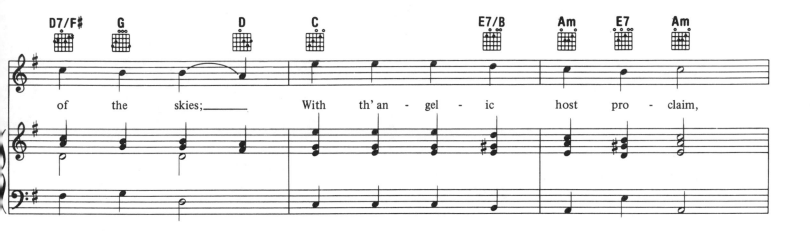

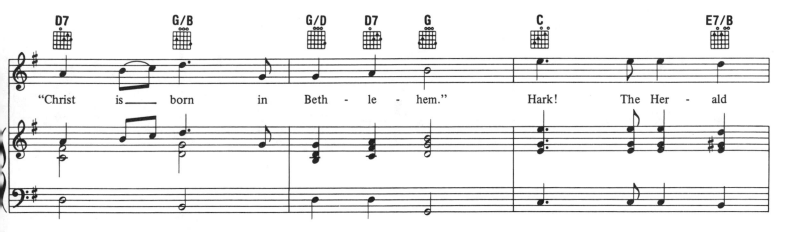

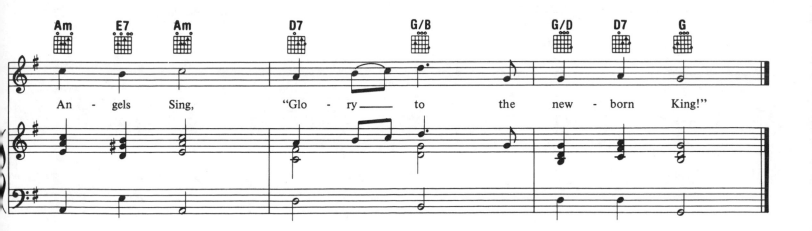

HE IS BORN, THE HOLY CHILD

French

3. Jesus, Lord of all the world,
   Coming as a child among us,
   Jesus, Lord of all the world,
   Grant to us Thy heav'nly peace.
   Refrain

HERE WE COME A-WASSAILING

English

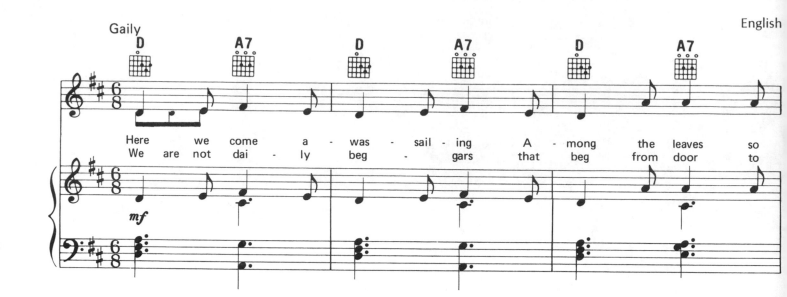

Here we come a-was-sail-ing A-mong the leaves so
We are not dai-ly beg-gars A that beg the from door to

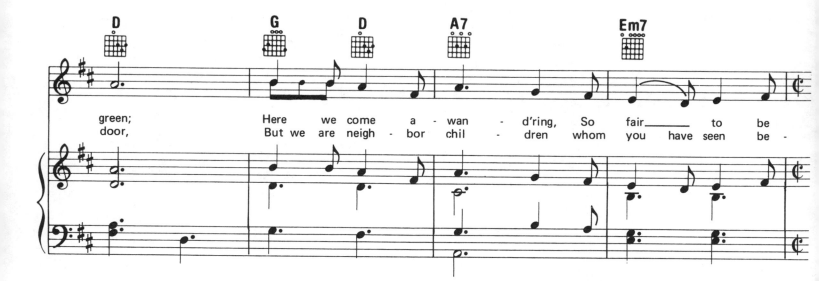

green; Here we come a-wan-d'ring, So fair____ to be
door, But we are neigh-bor chil-dren whom you have seen be-

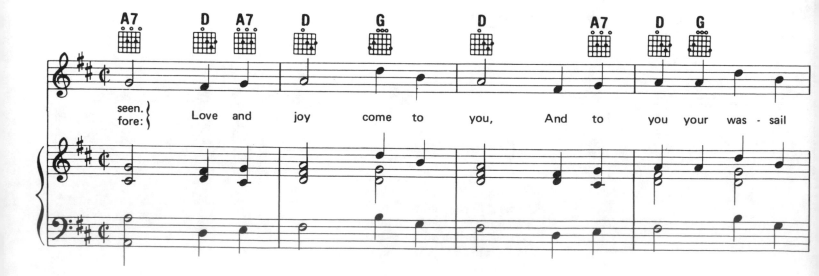

seen.
fore: Love and joy come to you, And to you your was-sail

3. We have got a little purse
   Of stretching leather skin;
   We want a little money
   To line it well within:

4. God bless the master of this house,
   Likewise the mistress too;
   And all the little children
   That round the table go:

THE HOLLY AND THE IVY

French

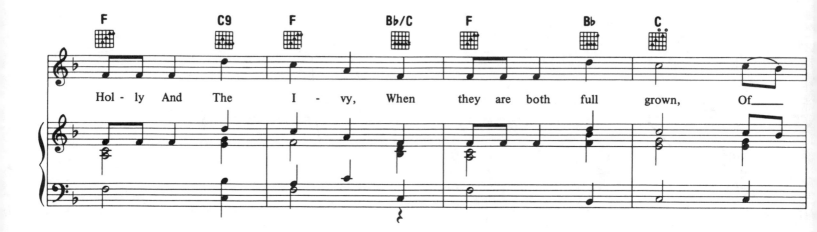

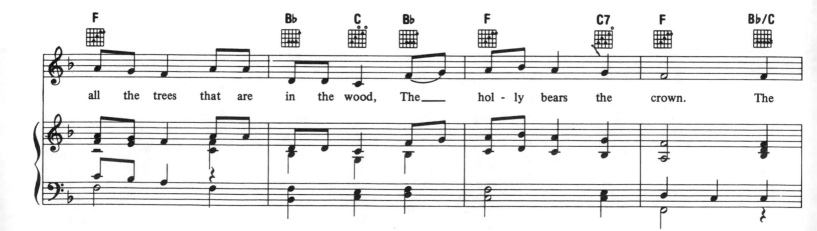

ris - ing of the sun____ And the run - ning of the deer, The ____

play - ing of the mer - ry or - gan, sweet sing - ing of the choir.

2. The holly bears a blossom,
   As white as lily flow'r,
   And Mary bore sweet Jesus Christ,
   To be our sweet Saviour.

   Refrain

3. The holly bears a berry,
   As red as any blood,
   And Mary bore sweet Jesus Christ,
   To do poor sinners good.

   Refrain

I AM SO GLAD ON CHRISTMAS EVE

Flowing

By PEDER KNUDSEN

Am So Glad____ On Christ - mas Eve, The night of Je - sus'
Am So Glad____ On Christ - mas Eve, My night prais - es rise____ a -

birth;_____ That's when a star____ shone like the sun, And
bove____ To when Je - sus Who____ has brought to earth The

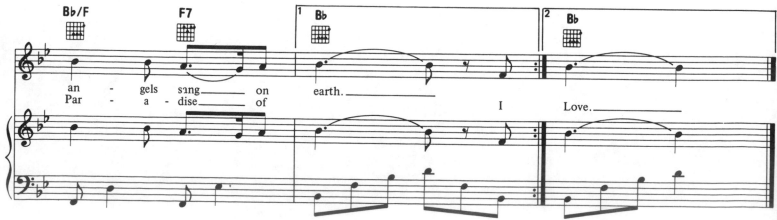

an - gels sang____ on earth._____
Par - a - dise of

I Love._____

I HEARD THE BELLS ON CHRISTMAS DAY

Words by HENRY WADSWORTH LONGFELLOW
Music by JOHN BAPTISTE CALKIN

3. And in despair I bow'd my head:
"There is no peace on earth," I said,
"For hate is strong, and mocks the song
Of peace on earth, good will to men."

4. Then pealed the bells more loud and deep:
"God is not dead, nor doth He sleep;
The wrong shall fail, the right prevail,
With peace on earth, good will to men."

5. Till, ringing, singing on its way,
The world revolved from night to day,
A voice, a chime, a chant sublime,
Of peace on earth, good will to men!

I SAW THREE SHIPS

English

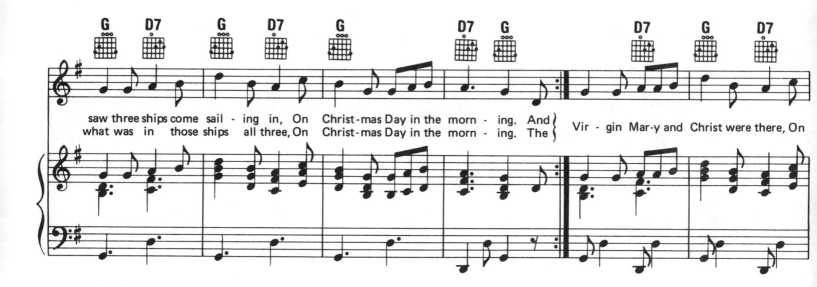

I saw three ships come sail - ing in, On Christ - mas Day, on Christ - mas Day; I
what was in those ships all three, On Christ - mas Day, on Christ - mas Day; And

saw three ships come sail - ing in, On Christ - mas Day in the morn - ing. And
what was in those ships all three, On Christ - mas Day in the morn - ing. The
Vir - gin Mar - y and Christ were there, On

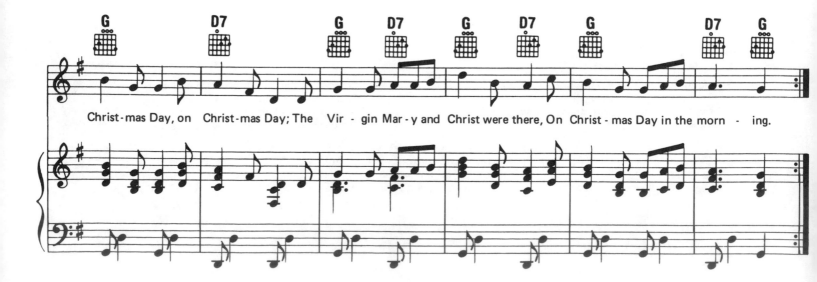

Christ - mas Day, on Christ - mas Day; The Vir - gin Mar - y and Christ were there, On Christ - mas Day in the morn - ing.

IN THE SILENCE OF THE NIGHT

IT CAME UPON THE MIDNIGHT CLEAR

Words by EDMUND H. SEARS
Music by RICHARD S. WILLIS

Quietly

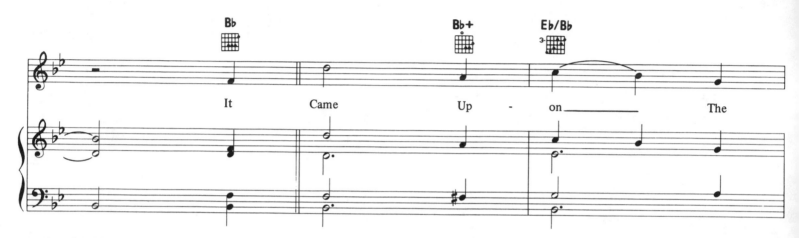

It Came Up - on _____ The Mid - night Clear, That glo - rious

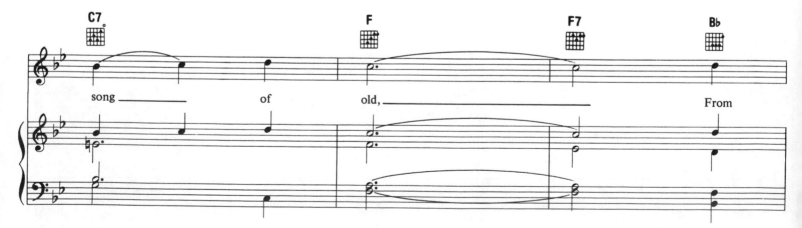

song _____ of old, _____ From

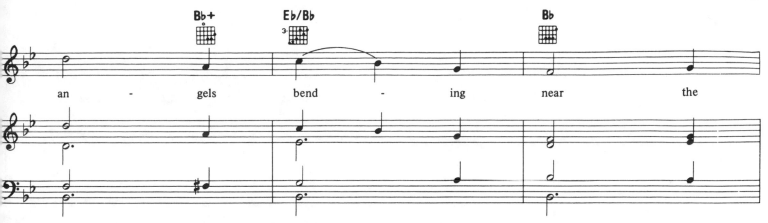

an - gels bend - ing near the

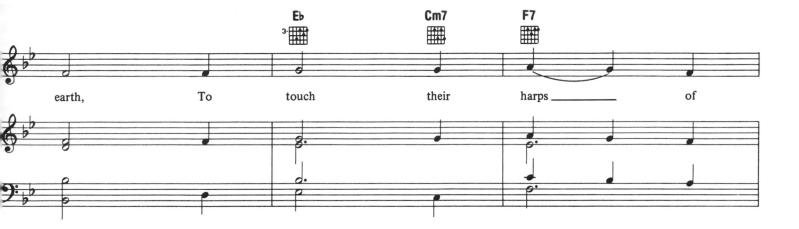

earth, To touch their harps _____ of

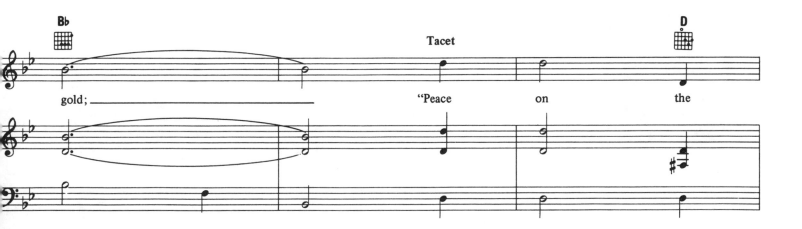

gold; _____ "Peace on the

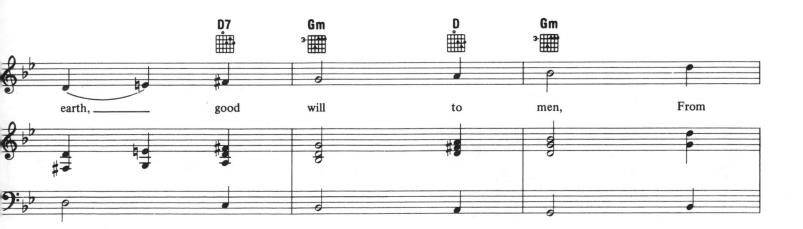

earth, _____ good will to men, From

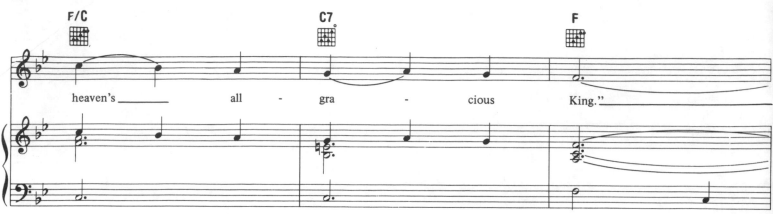

heaven's _____ all - gra - cious King." _____

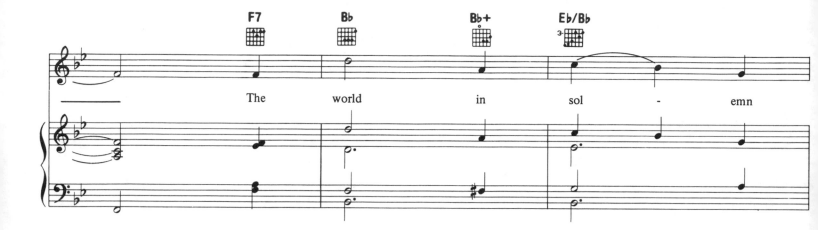

_____ The world in sol - emn

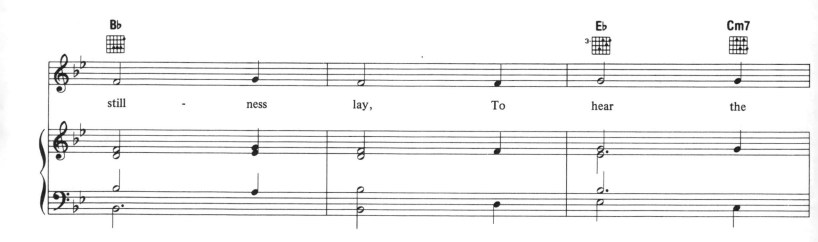

still - ness lay, To hear the

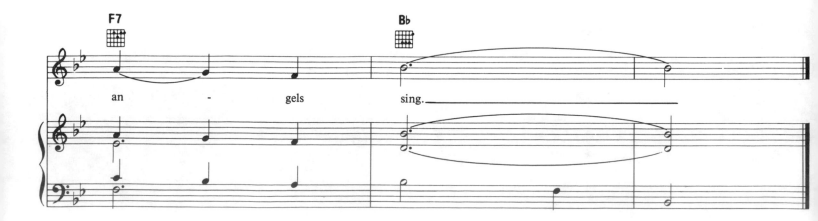

an - gels sing. _____

JESU, JOY OF MAN'S DESIRING

By J.S. BACH

Evenly

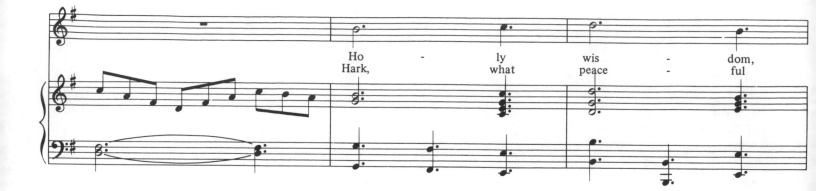

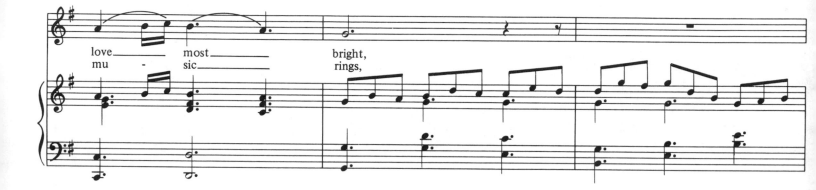

Ho - ly wis - dom,
Hark, what peace - ful

love_____ most_____ bright,
mu - sic_____ rings,

Drawn by the
Where the

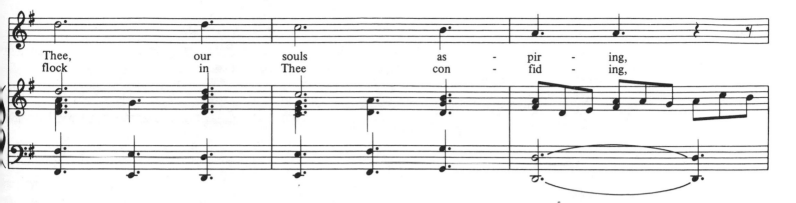

Thee, our souls as - pir - ing,
flock in Thee con - fid - ing,

Soar to of un - cre -
Drink of joy from

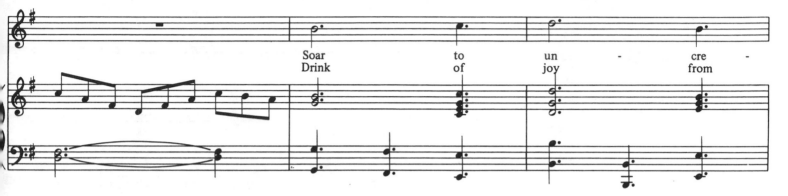

at - ed _____ light.
death - less _____ springs.

Word   of   God   our   flesh   that
Theirs   is   beau - ty's   fair - est

fash - ioned,
plea - sure,

With   the   fire   of   life   im -
Theirs   is   wis - dom's   ho - liest

pas - sioned.
trea - sure.

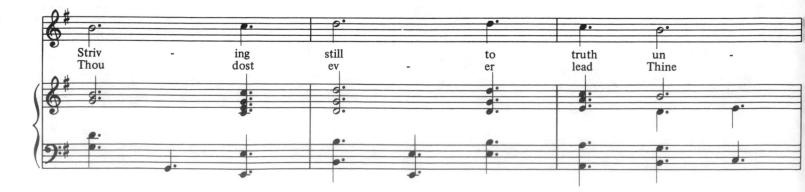

Striv - ing   still   to   truth   un -
Thou   dost   ev - er   lead   Thine

known,
own,
Soar - ing
In the

dy - ing
love of
round Thy
joys un - throne.
known.

JESUS HOLY, BORN SO LOWLY

Polish

Je - sus ho - ly, born so low - ly,
On the straw the Babe is sleep - ing,

We will sing you car - ols gay.
In the hum - ble man - ger bed.

Je - sus dear - est, pre - cious In - fant,
Ma - ry lov - ing watch is keep - ing,

JINGLE BELLS

Words and Music by
J. PIERPONT

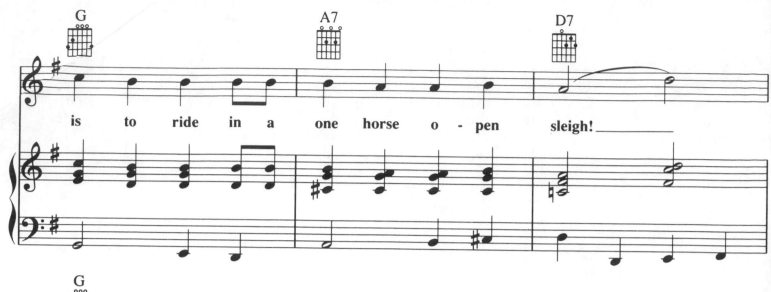

is to ride in a one horse o - pen sleigh! _____

Jin - gle Bells, Jin - gle Bells, jin - gle all the

way. Oh what fun it is to ride in a

one horse o - pen sleigh! A sleigh!

JOY TO THE WORLD

Words by Isaac Watts
Music by George F. Handel

With spirit

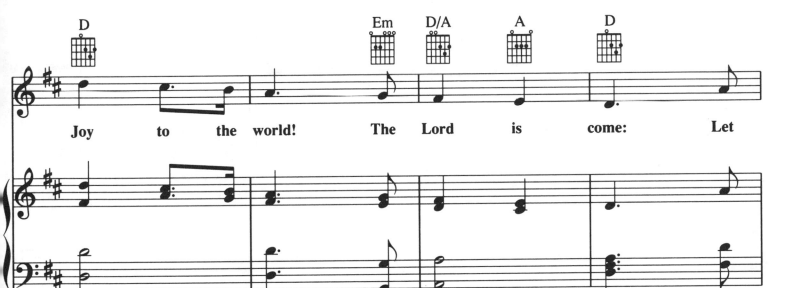

Joy to the world! The Lord is come: Let

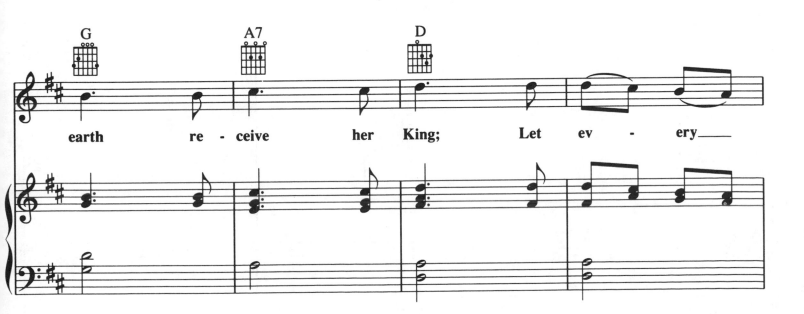

earth re - ceive her King; Let ev - ery____

heart _____ pre - pare _ Him _ room, _____ And heav - en and na - ture _

sing, _____ And _ heav - en and na - ture _ sing, _____ And _

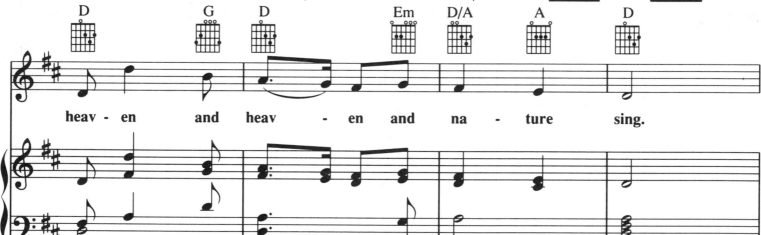

heav - en and heav - en and na - ture sing.

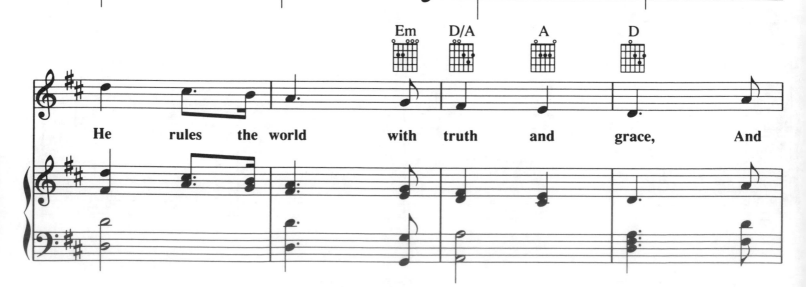

He rules the world with truth and grace, And

makes the na - tions prove The glo - ries _____

of _____ His right - eous - ness, _____ And won - ders of His ___

love, And ___ won - ders of His ___ love, And ___

won - ders, won - ders of His love.

JOLLY OLD ST. NICHOLAS

LITTLE CHILDREN, WAKE AND LISTEN

French

1. Lit - tle chil - dren, wake and lis - ten! Songs are
2. What is this that they are tell - ing Sing - ing

break - ing o'er the earth; While the stars in heav - en
in the qui - et street? While their voic - es high are

glis - ten, Hear the news of Je - sus' birth. Long a -
swell - ing, What sweet words do they re - peat? Words to

3. Christ has left His throne of glory,
   And a lowly cradle found;
   Well might angels tell the story,
   Well may we their words resound.
   Little children, wake and listen!
   Songs are ringing through the earth;
   While the stars in heaven glisten,
   Hail with joy your Saviour's birth.

LO, HOW A ROSE E'ER BLOOMING

By MICHAEL PRAETORIUS

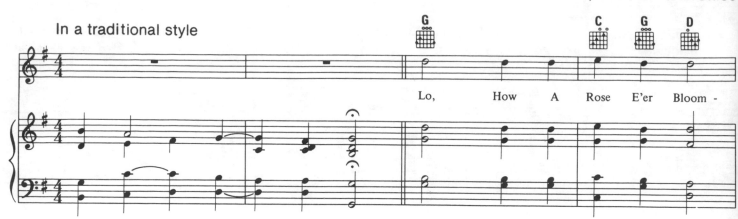

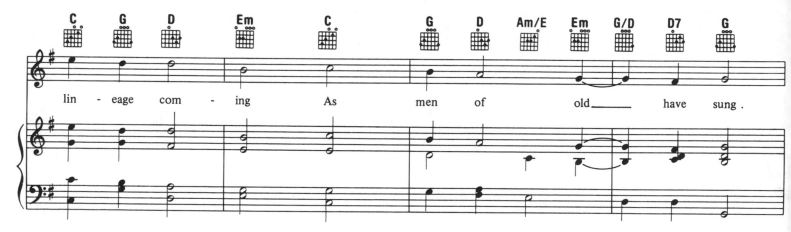

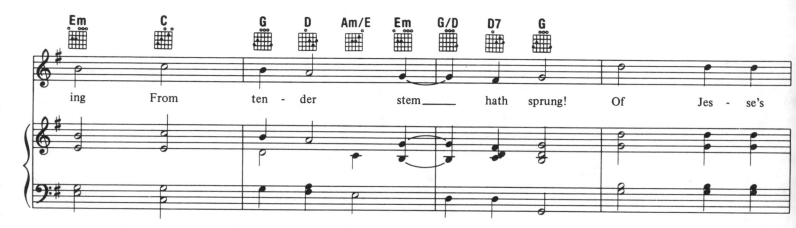

MARCH OF THE THREE KINGS

French

MARCH OF THE TOYS

With Spirit

By VICTOR HERBERT

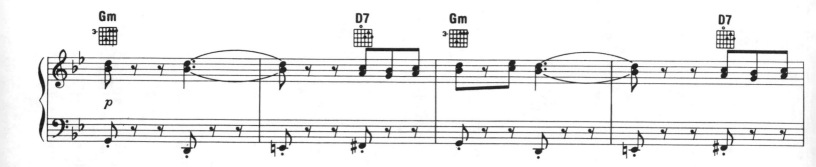

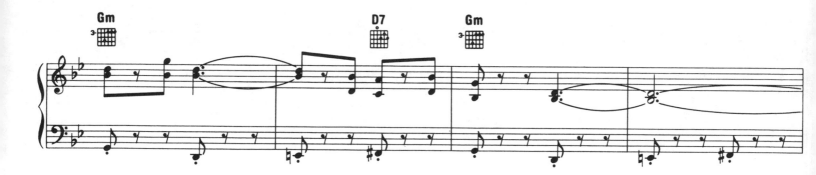

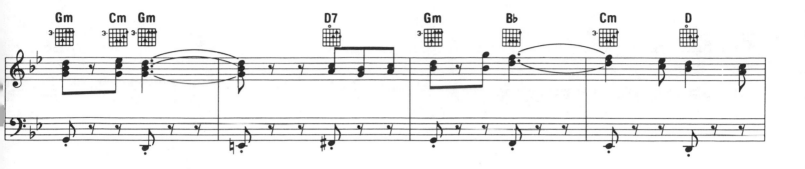

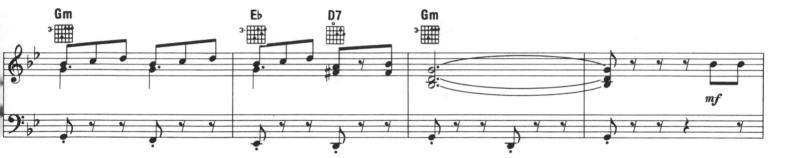

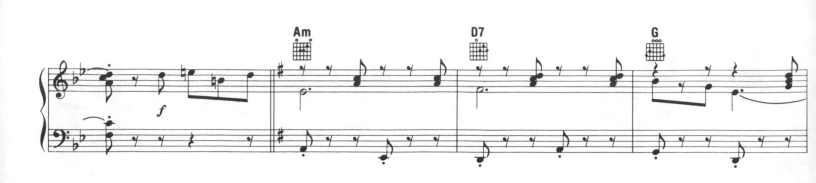

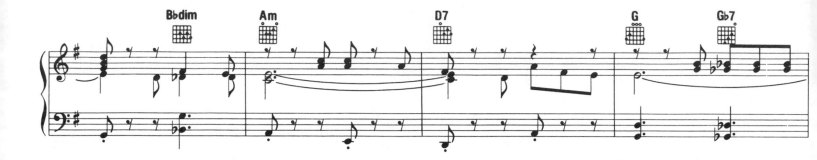

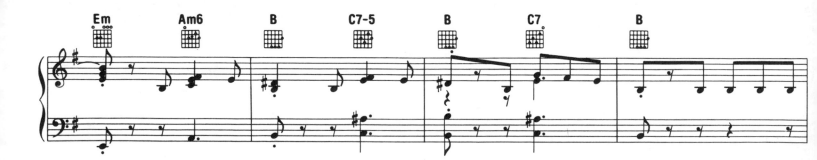

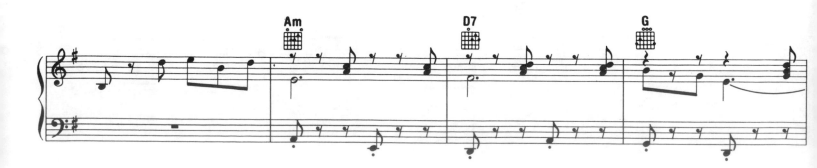

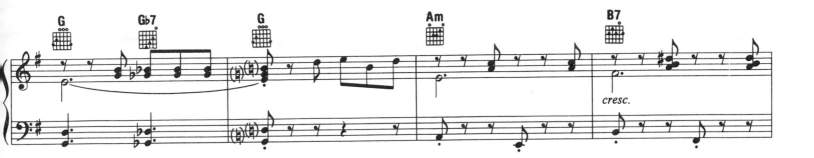

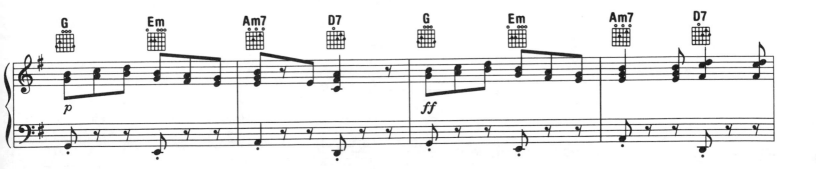

MARY HAD A BABY

African-American Spiritual

Flowing

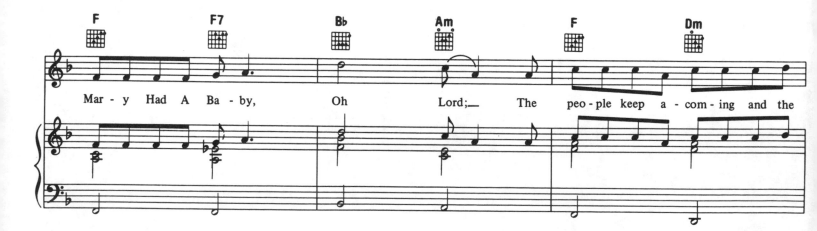

train__ done gone.

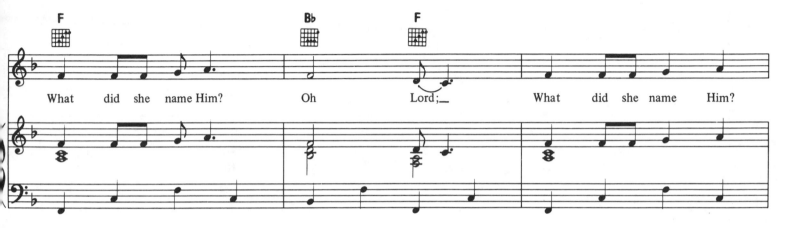

What did she name Him? Oh Lord;__ What did she name Him?

Oh my__ Lord; What did she name Him? Oh Lord;__ The

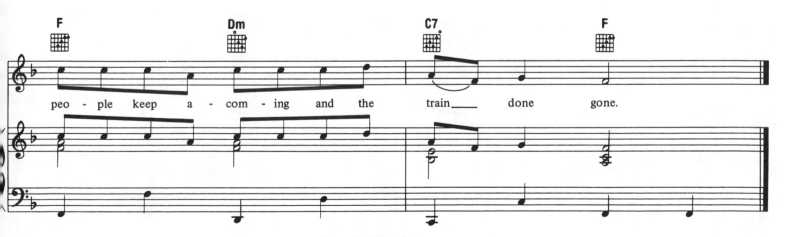

peo- ple keep a- com- ing and the train__ done gone.

She called Him Jesus. . .
Where was He born? . . .
Born in a stable. . .
Where did they lay Him? . . .
Laid Him in a manager. . .

NEIGHBOR, WHAT HAS YOU SO EXCITED?

French

"Neigh - bor, what has you so ex -
"It would be pleas - ant to go

ci - ted? Do tell me, please."
with you, Like - ly I'll go.

"Have - n't you heard? A Boy is
But can't we take our time to

O CHRISTMAS TREE

O COME ALL YE FAITHFUL

Latin Words translated by
FREDERICK OAKELEY
Music by JOHN READING

Triumphantly

O Come, All Ye Faith - ful,
Sing All choirs of an - gels,

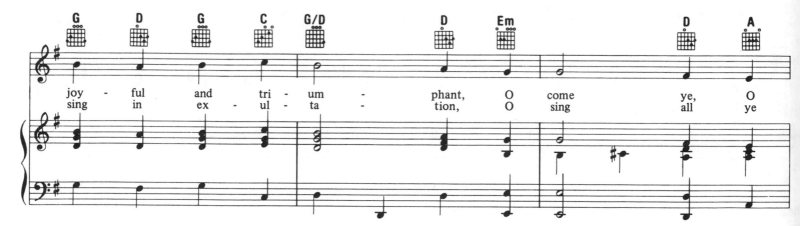

joy - ful and tri - um - phant, O come ye, O
sing in ex - ul - ta - tion, O come sing all ye

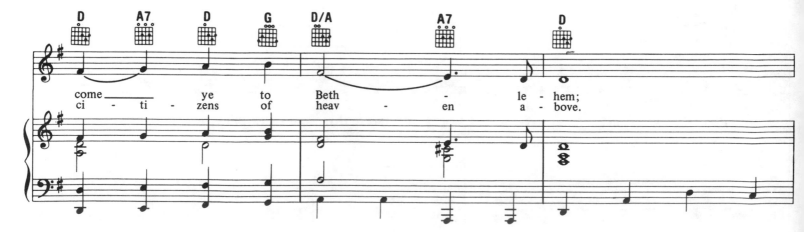

come ___ ye to Beth - le - hem;
ci - ti - zens of heav - en a - bove.

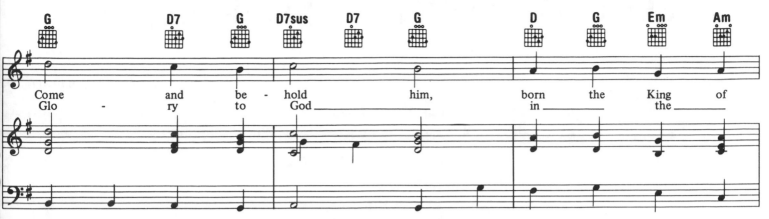

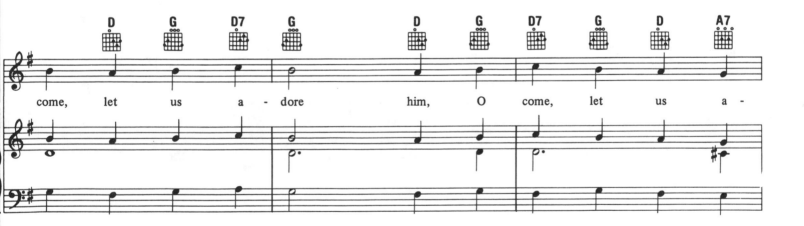

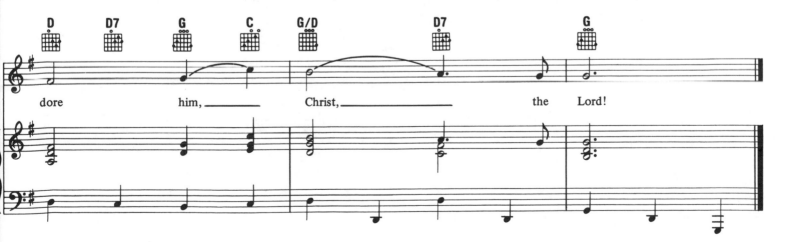

O COME AWAY, YE SHEPHERDS

18th Century French

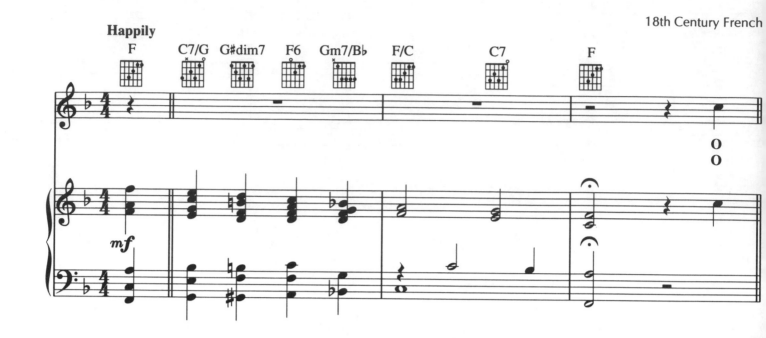

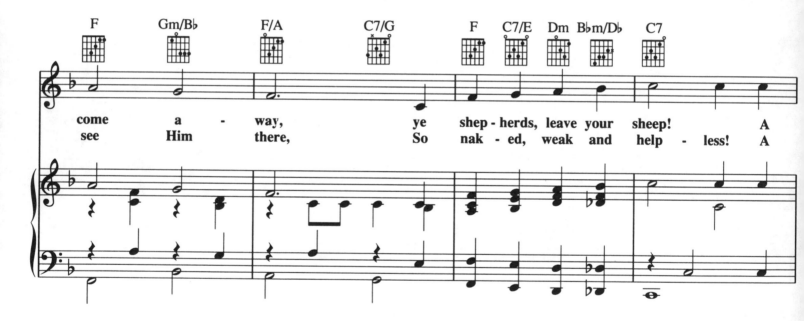

come a - way, ye shep-herds, leave your sheep! A
see Him there, So nak - ed, weak and help - less! A

King has come to ease our woe so deep! O
ti - ny babe With - in a man - ger laid. From

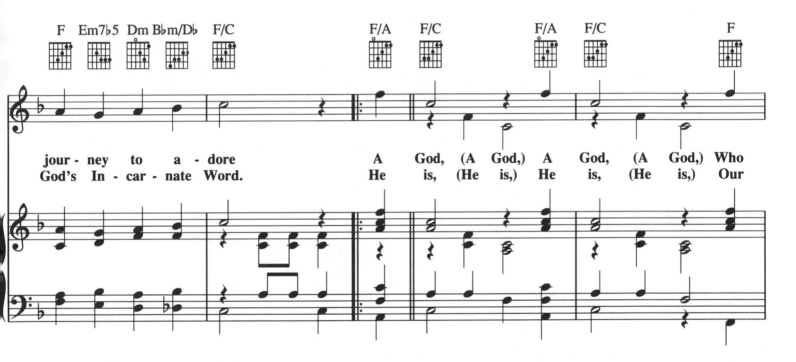

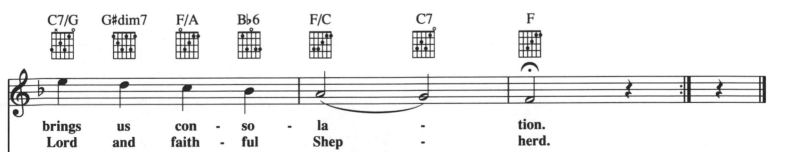

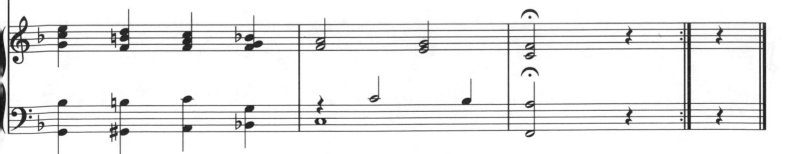

O COME, LITTLE CHILDREN

By J.A.P. SCHULZ

Quietly

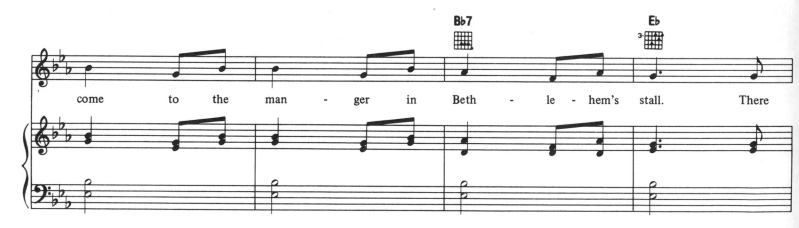

Come, Lit - tle Chil - dren, from cot and from hall, O

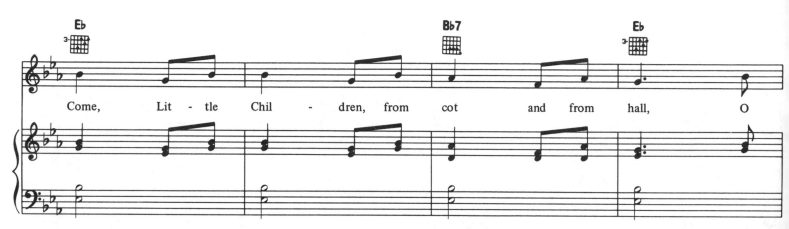

come to the man - ger in Beth - le - hem's stall. There

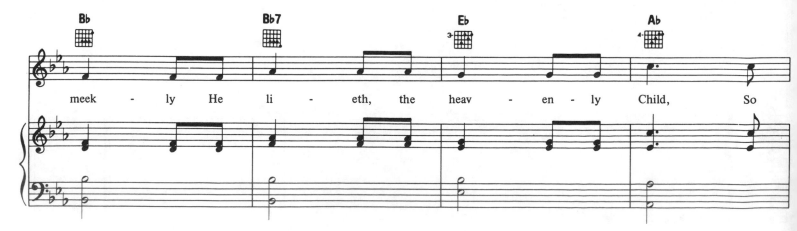

meek - ly He li - eth, the heav - en - ly Child, So

O COME, O COME, IMMANUEL

Plainsong, 13th Century
Words translated by JOHN M. NEALE and HENRY S. COFFIN

Like an old plainsong

O

Guitar tacet

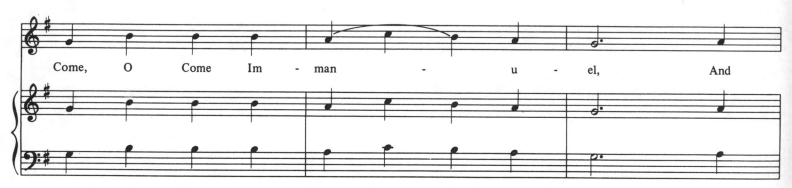

Come, O Come Im - man - u - el, And

ran - som cap - tive Is - ra - el, That mourns in lone - ly

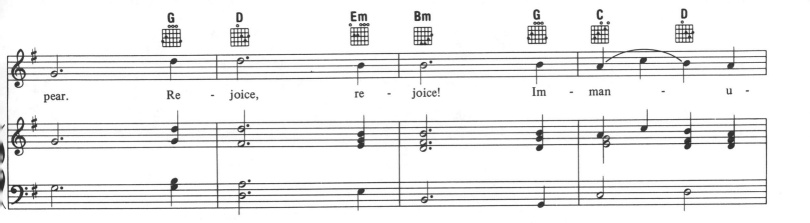

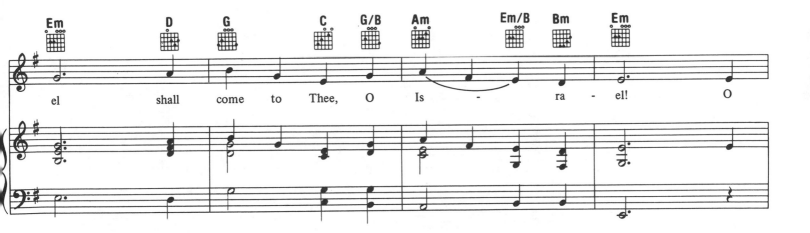

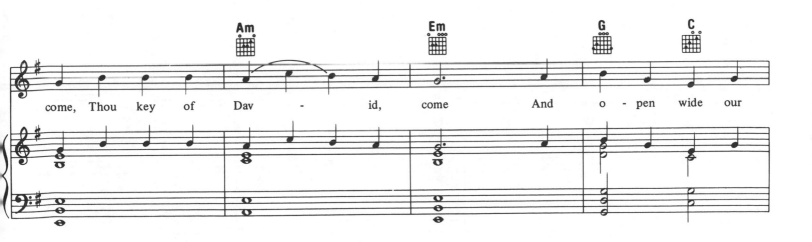

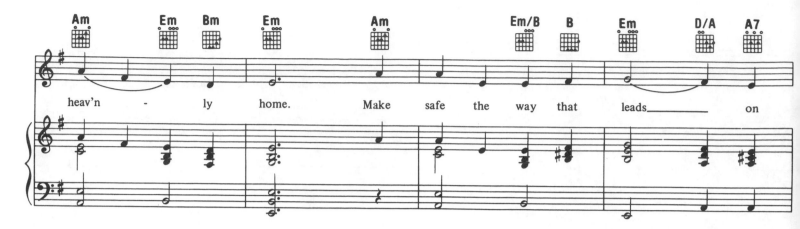

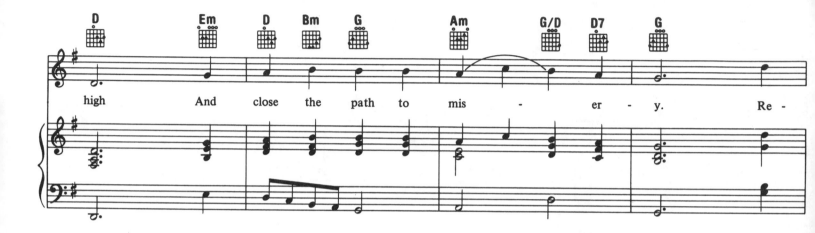

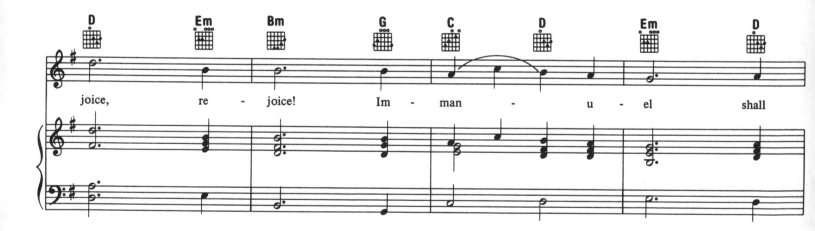

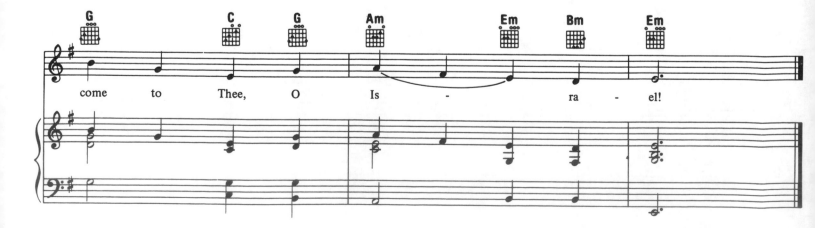

O LET US ALL BE GLAD TODAY

Words and Music by
MARTIN LUTHER

3. Twice welcome, O Thou heavenly guest,
   To save a world with sin distressed;
   Com'st Thou in lowly guise for me?
   What homage shall I give to Thee?

4. Ah! Lord eternal, heavenly King,
   Hast Thou become so mean a thing?
   And hast Thou left Thy blissful seat,
   To rest where colts and oxen eat?

5. Jesus, my Savior, come to me,
   Make here a little crib for Thee;
   A bed make in this heart of mine,
   That I may ay remember Thine.

6. Then from my soul glad songs shall ring;
   Of Thee each day I'll gladly sing;
   Then glad hosannas will I raise,
   From heart that loves to sing Thy praise.

O HOLY NIGHT

English Words by J.S. DWIGHT
Music by ADOLPHE ADAM

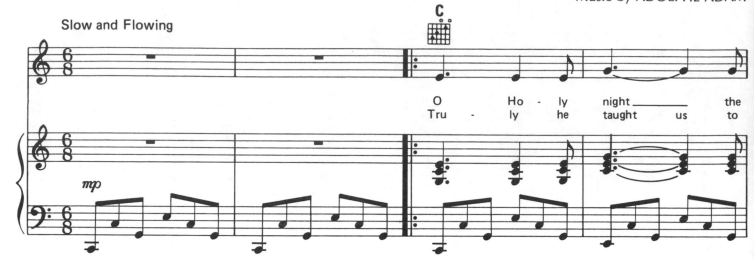

Slow and Flowing

O Ho - ly night _____ the
Tru - ly he taught us to

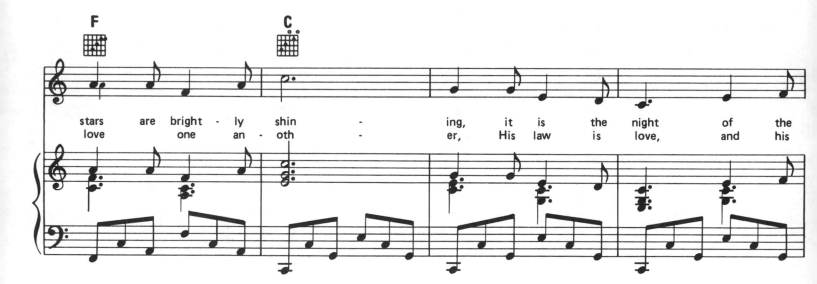

stars are bright - ly shin - - - ing, it is the night of the
love one an - oth - - - er, His law is love, and his

dear Sav - ior's birth; _____ Long lay the
gos - pel is peace; _____ Chains shall He

O LITTLE TOWN OF BETHLEHEM

Words by PHILLIPS BROOKS
Music by LEWIS H. REDNER

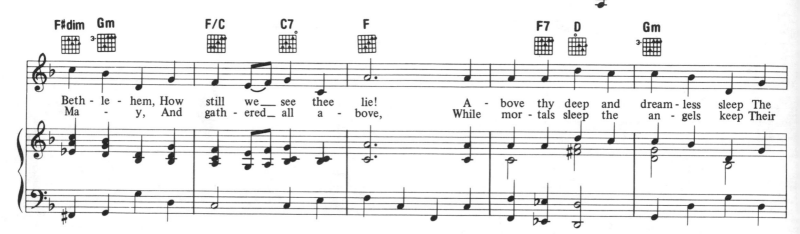

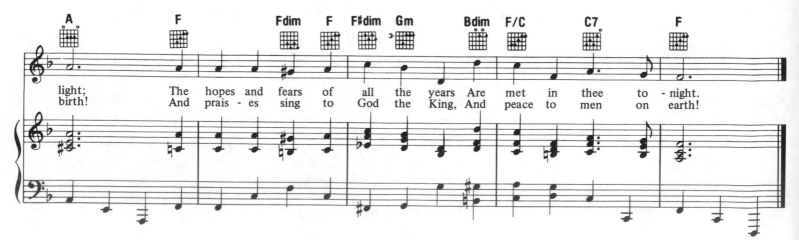

RISE UP, SHEPHERD AND FOI

O SANCTISSIMA

Sicilian

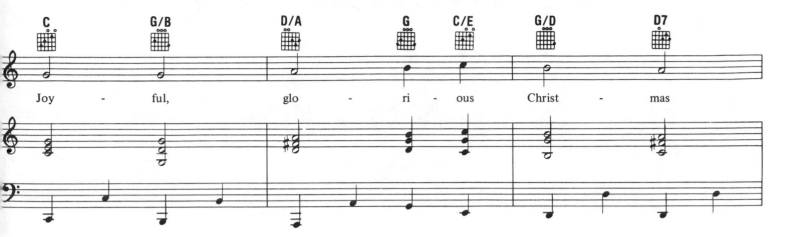

Joy - ful, glo - ri - ous Christ - mas

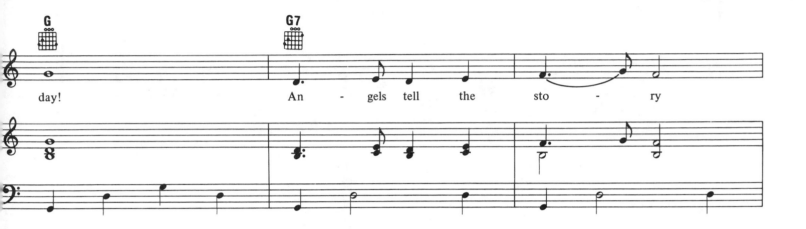

day! An - gels tell the sto - ry

of this day of glo - ry, Praise_____ Christ, our

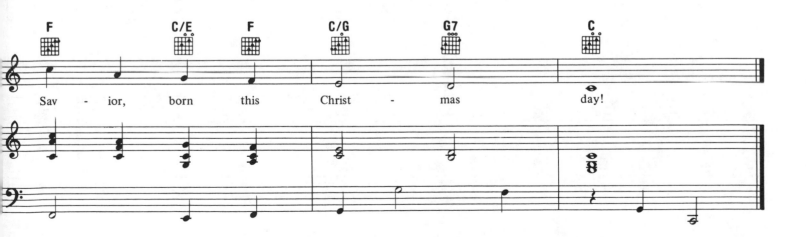

Sav - ior, born this Christ - mas day!

ON CHRISTMAS NIGHT

Sussex Carol

3. So how on earth can men be sad,
   When Jesus comes to make us glad?
   So how on earth can men be sad,
   When Jesus comes to make us glad?
   From all our sins to set us free,
   Buying for us our liberty.

4. From out the darkness have we light,
   Which makes the angels sing this night:
   From out the darkness have we light,
   Which makes the angels sing this night:
   "Glory to God, His peace to men,
   And good will, evermore! Amen."

ONCE IN ROYAL DAVID'S CITY

Words by C.F. ALEXANDER
Music by H.J. GAUNTLETT

Quietly

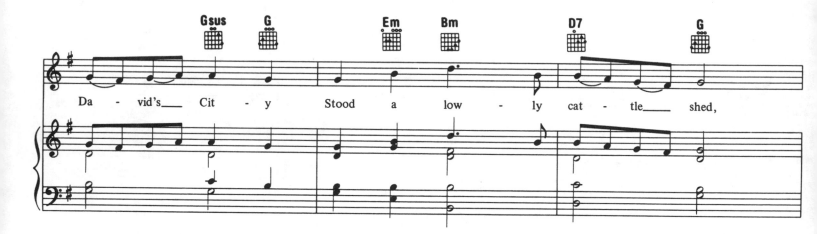

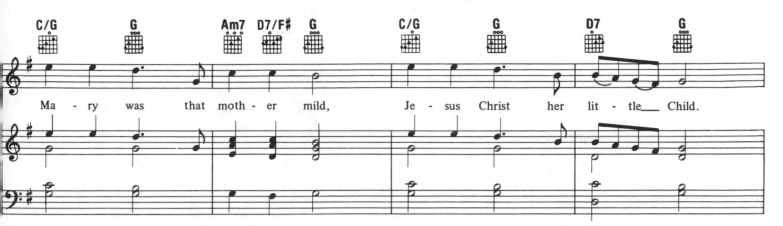

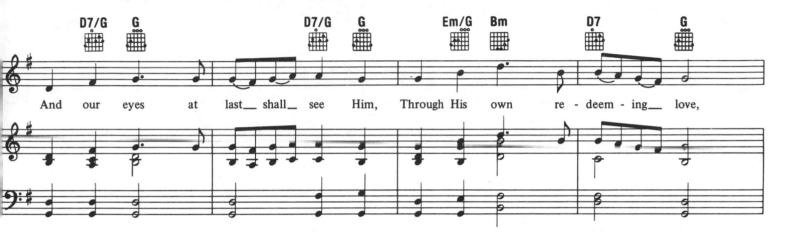

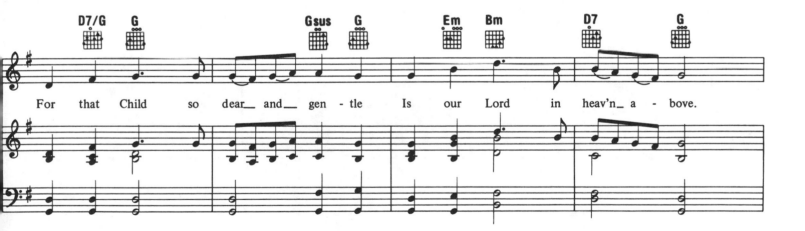

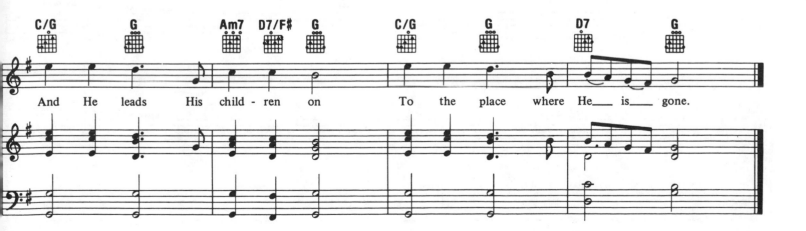

PAT-A-PAN
(Willie, Take Your Little Drum)

Words and Music by
BERNARD de la MONNOYE

155

3. God and man today become
Closely joined as flute and drum.
Let the joyous tune play on!
As the instruments you play,
We will sing, this Christmas day.

SHEPHERD, SHAKE OFF YOUR DROWSY SLEEP

French Besancon Carol

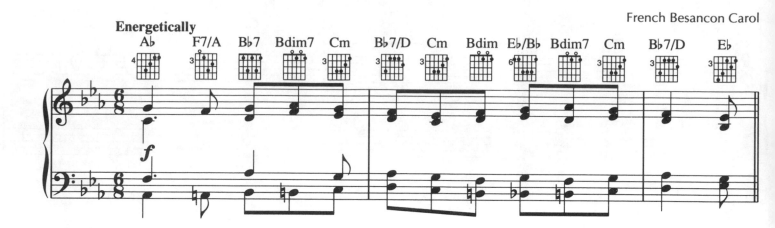

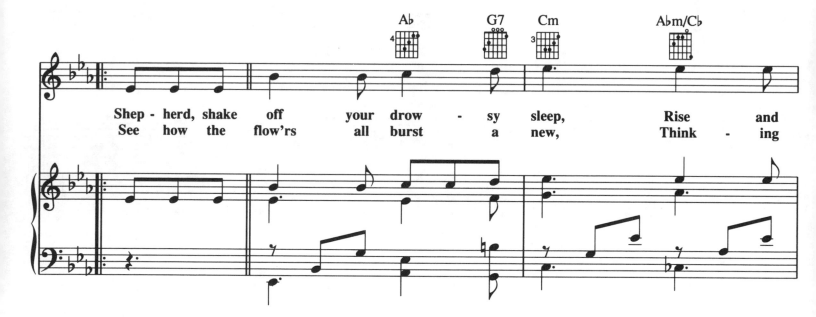

Shep - herd, shake off your drow - sy sleep, Rise and
See how the flow'rs all burst a new, Think - ing

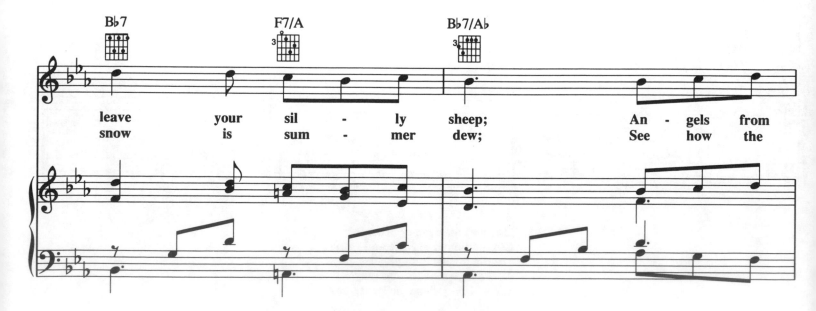

leave your sil - ly sheep; An - gels from
snow is sum - mer dew; See how the

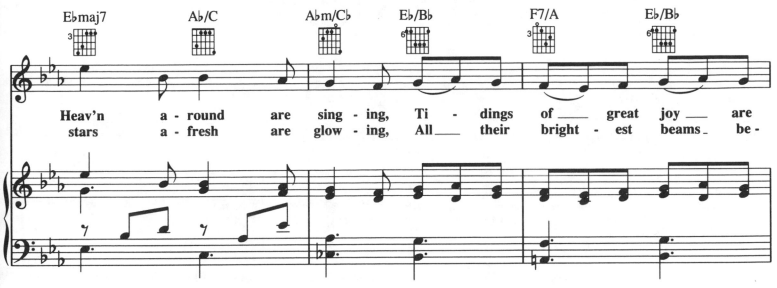

Heav'n a - round are sing - ing, Ti - dings of ____ great joy ____ are
stars a - fresh are glow - ing, All ____ their bright - est beams ____ be -

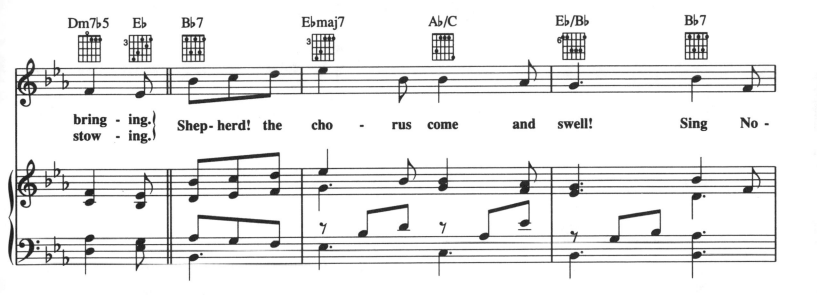

bring - ing.) Shep - herd! the cho - rus come and swell! Sing No -
stow - ing.)

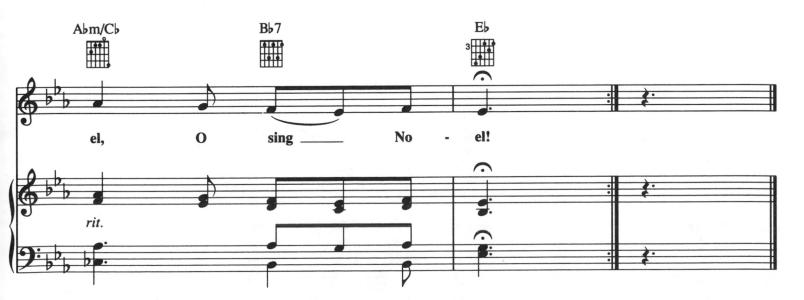

el, O sing _____ No - el!

rit.

3. Shepherd, then up and quick away!
Seek the Babe ere break of day.
He is the hope of ev'ry nation,
All in Him shall find salvation.

SILENT NIGHT

Words by JOSEPH MOHR
Music by FRANZ GRUBER

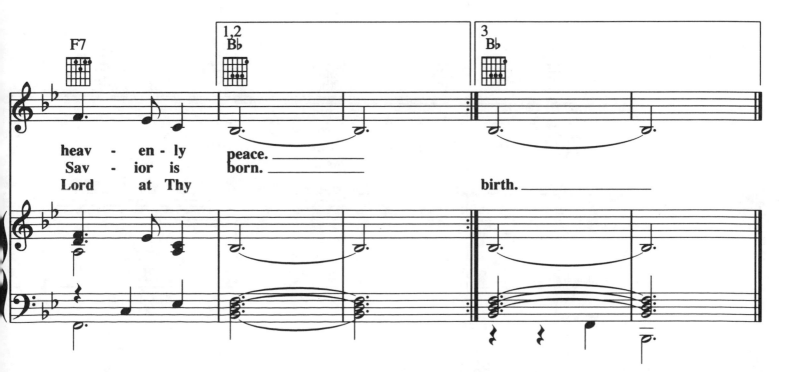

SING, O SING,
THIS BLESSED MORN

Words by CHRISTOPHER WORDSWORTH
German Folk

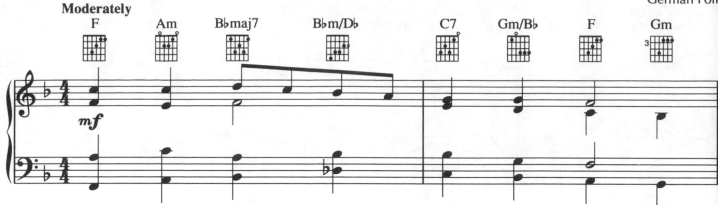

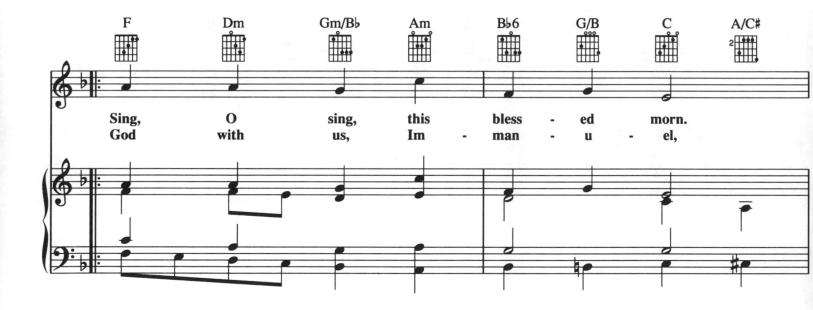

Sing, O sing, this bless - ed morn.
God with us, Im - man - u - el,

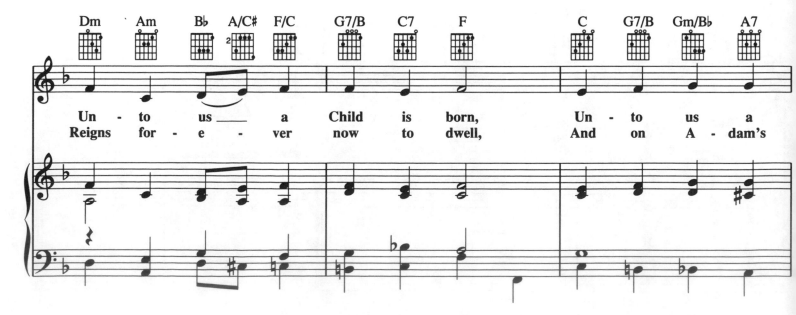

Un - to us ___ a Child is born, Un - to us a
Reigns for - e - ver now to dwell, And on A - dam's

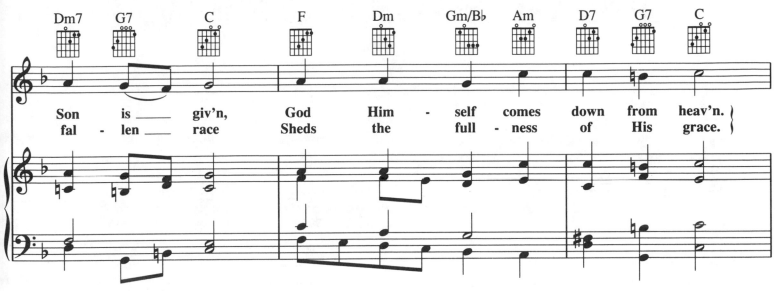

Son is ___ giv'n, God Him - self comes down from heav'n.
fal - len ___ race Sheds the full - ness of His grace.

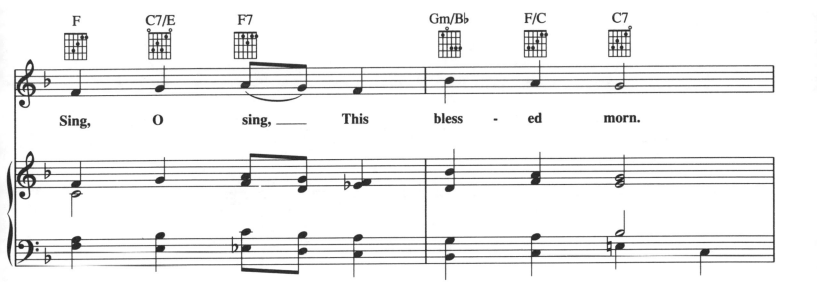

Sing, O sing, ___ This bless - ed morn.

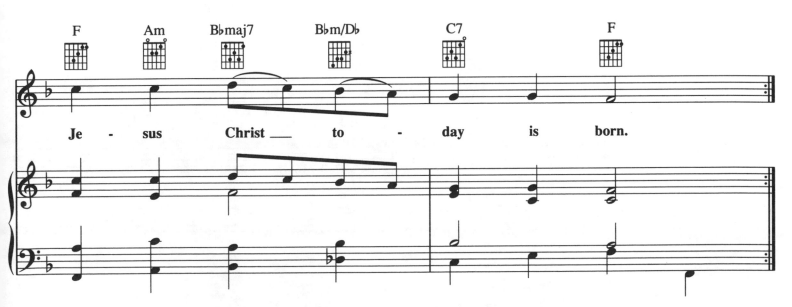

Je - sus Christ ___ to - day is born.

3. God comes down that man may rise,
   Lifted by Him to the skies;
   Christ is son of Man that we
   Son of God in Him may be:
   Refrain

4. O renew us, Lord, we pray,
   With Thy spirit day by day;
   That we ever one may be
   With the Father and with Thee:
   Refrain

SING WE NOW OF CHRISTMAS

Joyfully

French

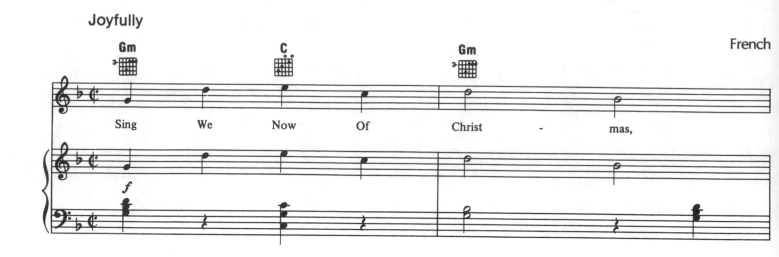

Sing We Now Of Christ - mas,

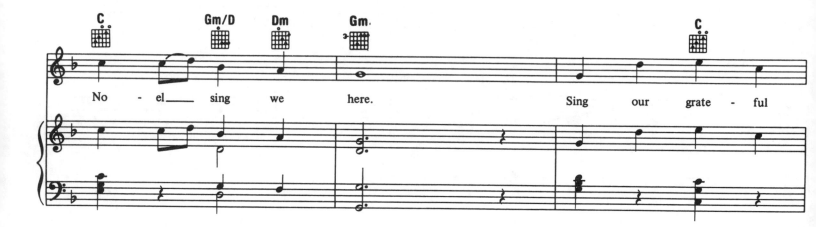

No - el sing we here. Sing our grate - ful

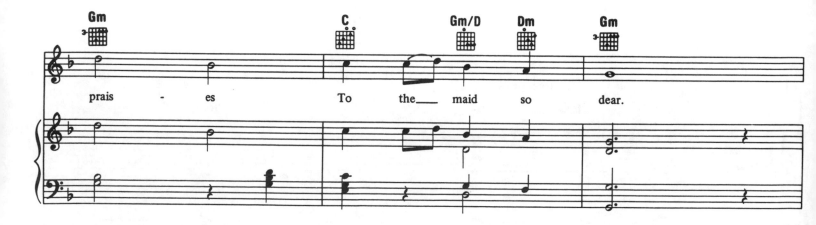

prais - es To the maid so dear.

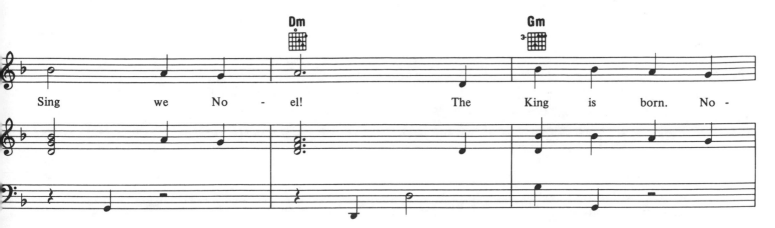

Sing we No - el! The King is born. No -

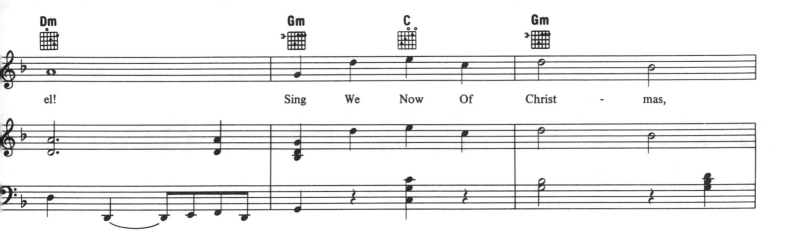

el! Sing We Now Of Christ - mas,

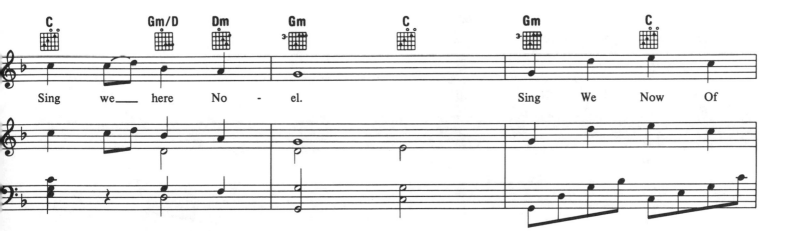

Sing we___ here No - el. Sing We Now Of

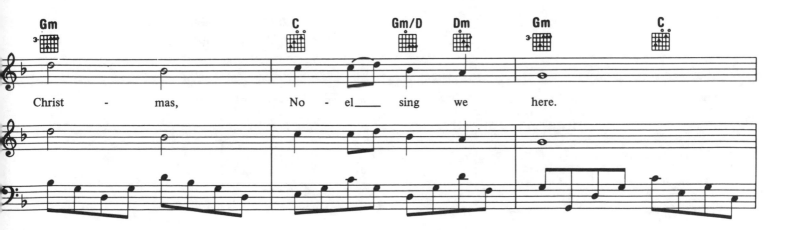

Christ - mas, No - el___ sing we here.

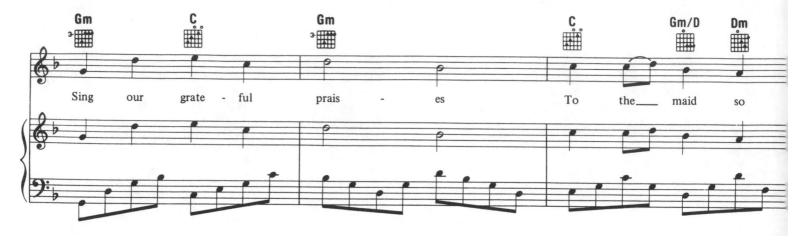

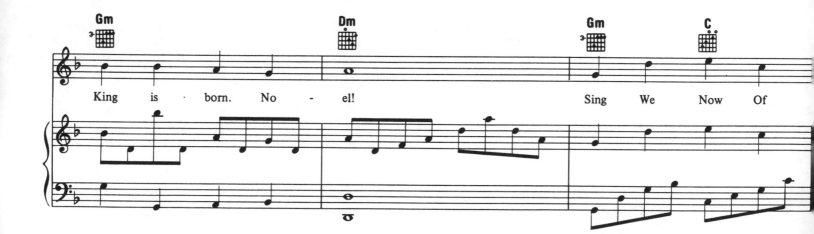

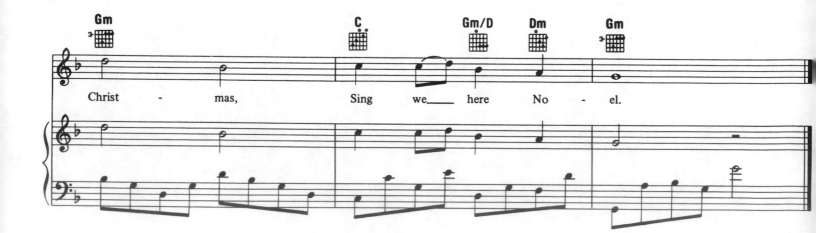

'TWAS THE NIGHT BEFORE CHRISTMAS

Words by CLEMENT CLARK MOORE
Music by F. HENRI KLICKMAN

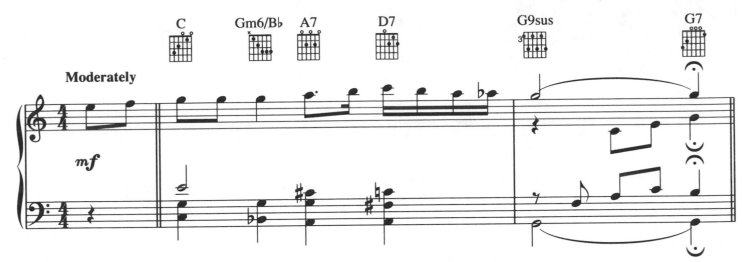

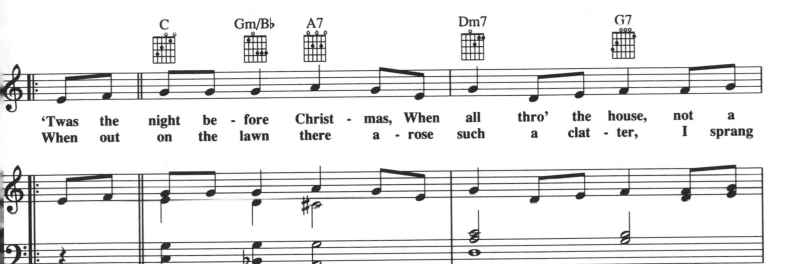

'Twas the night be - fore Christ - mas, When all thro' the house, not a
When out on the lawn there a - rose such a clat - ter, I sprang

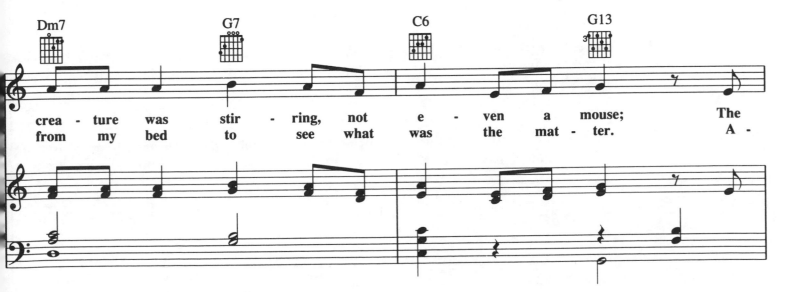

crea - ture was stir - ring, not e - ven a mouse; The
from my bed to see what was the mat - ter. A -

3. With a little old driver, so lively and quick,
I knew in a moment it must be St. Nick.
More rapid than eagles his coursers they came,
And he whistled, and shouted, and called them by name:
"Now, Dasher! now, Dancer now, Prancer! now Vixen
On, Comet! on, Cupid! on Donder and Blitzen!
To the top of the porch, to the top of the wall!
Now dash away, dash away, dash away all!"

4. As dry leaves that before the wild hurricane fly,
When they meet with an obstacle, mount to the sky,
So up to top house-top the coursers they flew,
With the sleigh full of toys, and St. Nicholas, too.
And then in a twinkling I heard on the roof
The prancing and pawing of each little hoof.
As I drew in my head, and was turning around,
Down the chimney St. Nicholas came with a bound.

5. He was dressed all in fur from head to his foot,
And his clothes were all tarnished with ashes and soot;
A bundle of toys he had flung on his back,
And he look like a peddler just opening his pack
His eyes how they twinkled! his dimples how merry!
His cheeks were like roses, his noses like a cherry,
His droll little mouth was drawn up like a bow,
And the beard of his chin was as white as the snow.

6. The stump of a pipe he held tight in his teeth,
And the smoke, it encircled his head like a wreath.
He had a broad face, and a round little belly
That shook, when he laughed, like a bowl full of jelly.
He was chubby and plump - a right jolly old elf -
And I laughed when I saw him, in spite of myself.
A wink of his eye, and a twist of his head,
Soon gave me to know I had nothing to dread.

7. He spoke not a word, but went straight to his work,
And filled all the stockings; then turned with a jerk,
And laying his finger aside of his nose,
And giving a nod, up the chimney he rose.
He sprang to his sleigh, to his team gave a whistle,
And away they all fled like the down of a thistle;
But I heard him exclaim, ere he drove out of sight -
"Happy Christmas to all, and to all a Good-night!"

SLEEP, O SLEEP, MY LOVELY CHILD

Italian

Slowly with expression

Sleep,   o sleep,   my   love - ly   Child,
O   my   trea - sure   do   not   weep!

King   di - vine,   King   di - vine.   Close your
Sweet - ly ___ sleep,   sweet - ly ___ sleep.   Close your

eyes   and   sweet - ly   slum -   ber,   King   di -
eyes   and   my   Son,   ly   my   dear   one.   Sweet - ly

STILL, STILL, STILL

THE THREE KINGS SONG

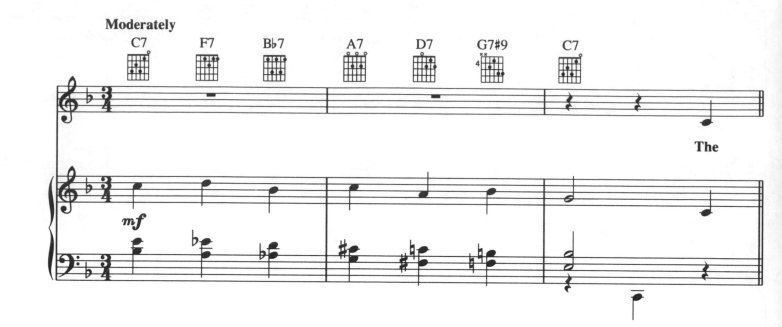

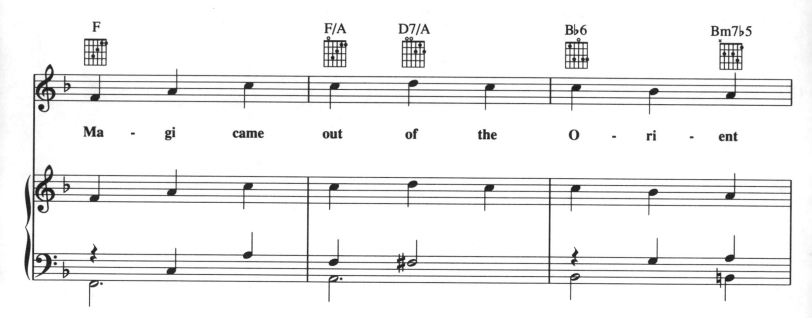

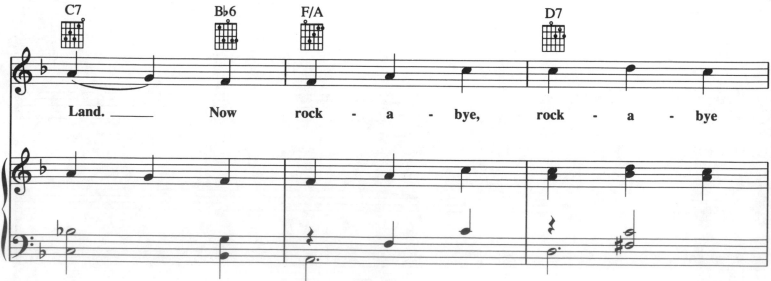

THE TWELVE DAYS OF CHRISTMAS

Traditional

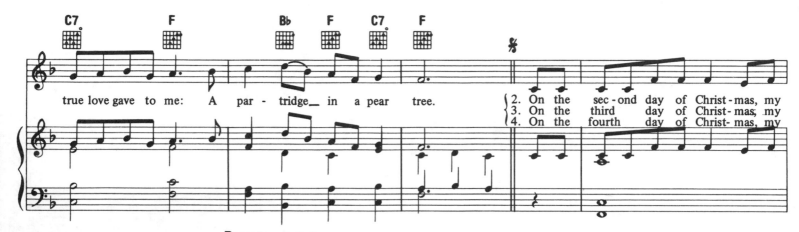

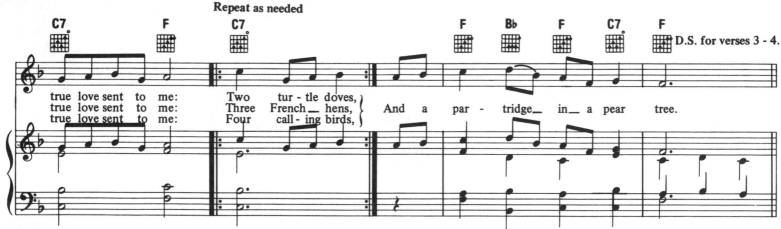

rings.   Four____ call - ing birds, Three   French   hens,

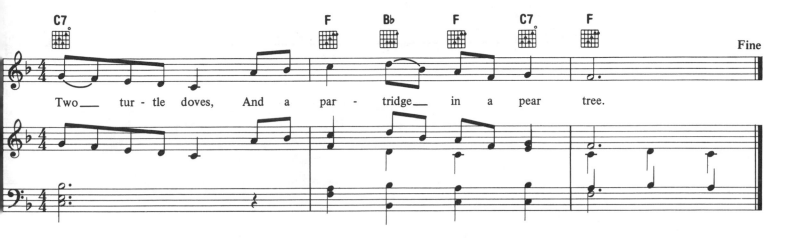

Two____ tur - tle doves, And a par - tridge__ in a pear   tree.

Fine

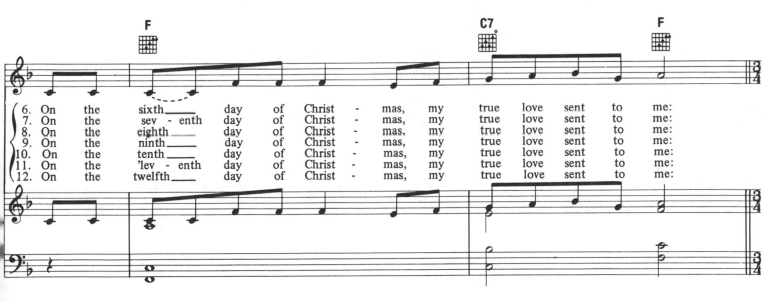

6. On the sixth____ day of Christ - mas, my true love sent to me:
7. On the sev - enth day of Christ - mas, my true love sent to me:
8. On the eighth____ day of Christ - mas, my true love sent to me:
9. On the ninth____ day of Christ - mas, my true love sent to me:
10. On the tenth____ day of Christ - mas, my true love sent to me:
11. On the 'lev - enth day of Christ - mas, my true love sent to me:
12. On the twelfth____ day of Christ - mas, my true love sent to me:

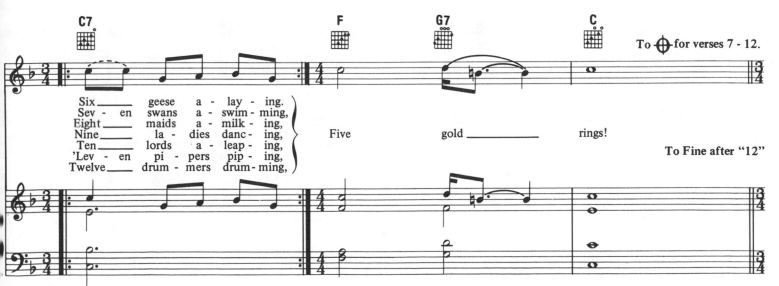

Six____ geese a - lay - ing.
Sev - en swans a - swim - ming,
Eight____ maids a - milk - ing,
Nine____ la - dies danc - ing,
Ten____ lords a - leap - ing,
'Lev - en pi - pers pip - ing,
Twelve____ drum - mers drum - ming,

Five   gold_____ rings!

To ⊕ for verses 7 - 12.

To Fine after "12"

UP ON THE HOUSETOP

Traditional

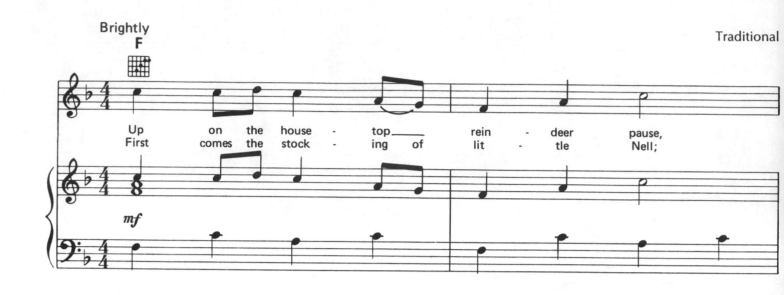

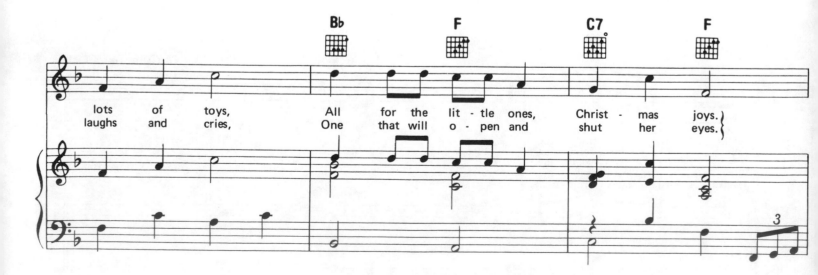

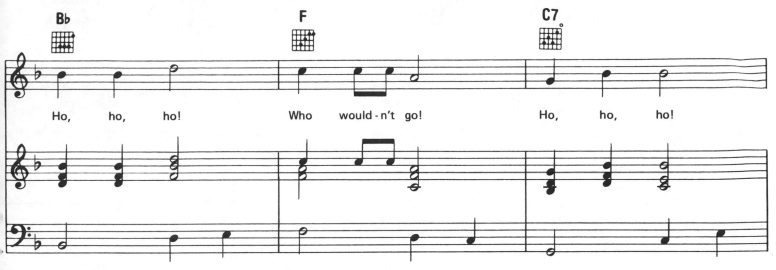

Ho, ho, ho! Who would-n't go! Ho, ho, ho!

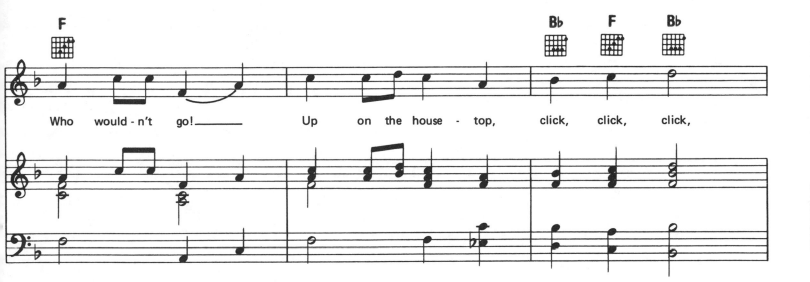

Who would-n't go!___ Up on the house-top, click, click, click,

Down thru the chim-ney with good Saint Nick.

WATCHMAN, TELL US OF THE NIGHT

Words by JOHN BOWRING
Music by JAKOB HINTZE

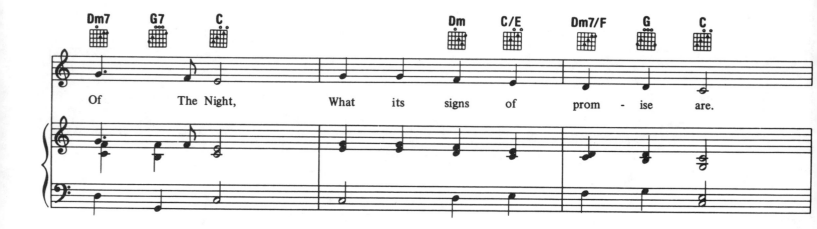

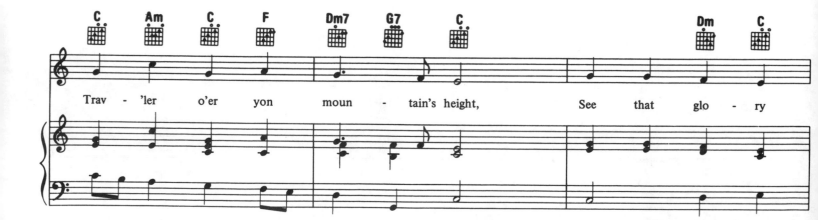

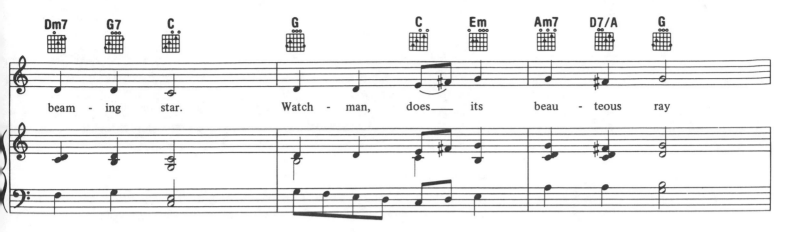

beam - ing star. Watch - man, does___ its beau - teous ray

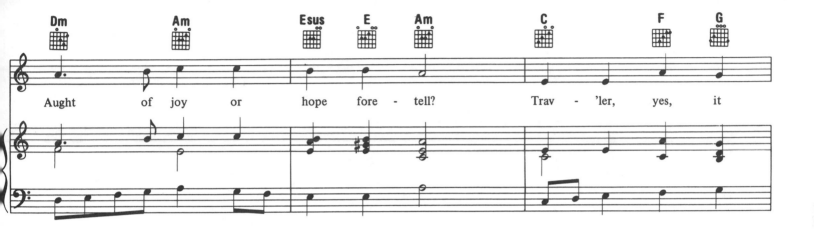

Aught of joy or hope fore - tell? Trav - 'ler, yes, it

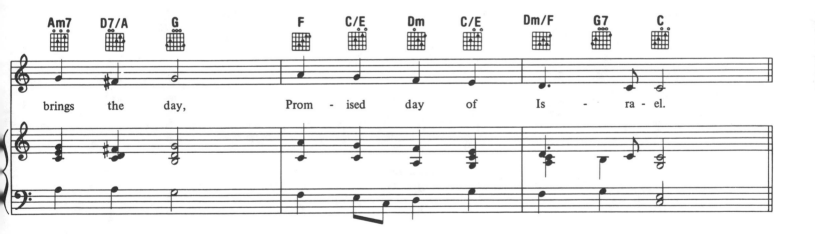

brings the day, Prom - ised day of Is - ra - el.

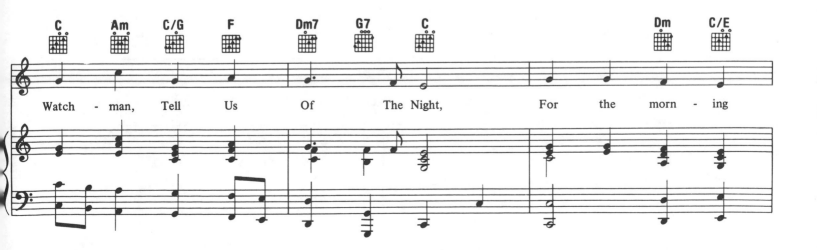

Watch - man, Tell Us Of The Night, For the morn - ing

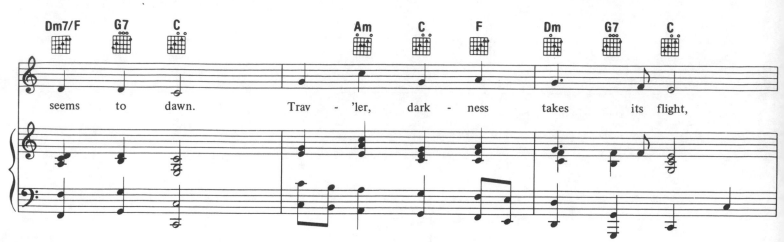

seems to dawn. Trav - 'ler, dark - ness takes its flight,

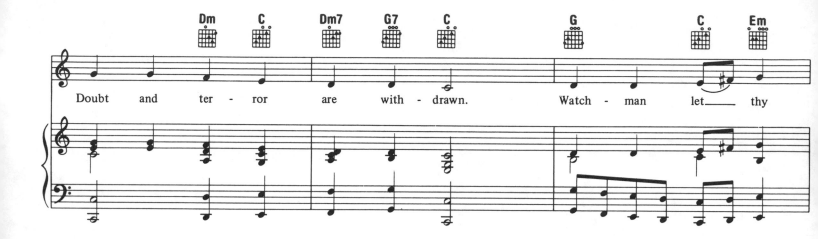

Doubt and ter - ror are with - drawn. Watch - man let____ thy

wand - 'rings cease, Hie thee to thy qui - et home.

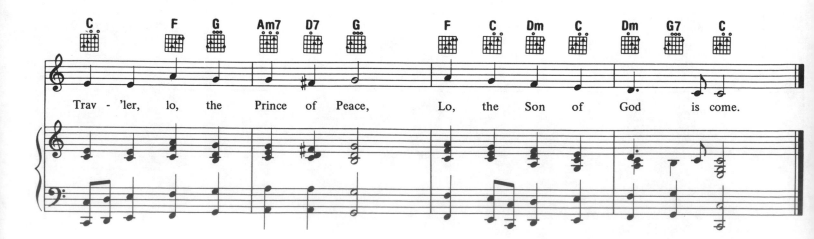

Trav - 'ler, lo, the Prince of Peace, Lo, the Son of God is come.

WE WISH YOU A MERRY CHRISTMAS

English

WE THREE KINGS OF ORIENT ARE

Words and Music by
JOHN H. HOPKINS

Moderately

We Three Kings of O - ri - ent are;

Bear - ing gifts we tra - verse a - far,

Field and foun - tain, moor and moun - tain,

WHAT CHILD IS THIS?

English

Slow and Serene

What Child is this,_____ who, laid to rest,_____ On
So bring Him in - cense, gold and myrrh,_____ Come

Ma - ry's lap_____ is sleep - ing? Whom an - gels
peas - ant king_____ to own Him; The King of

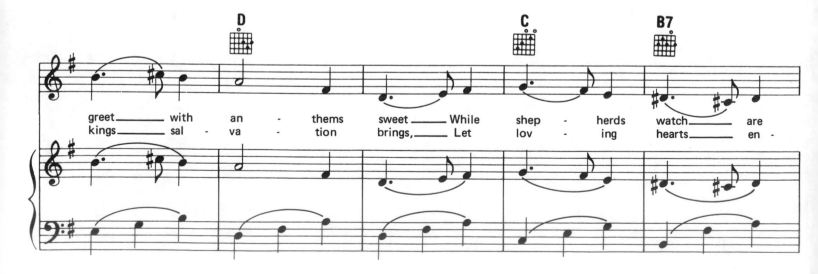

greet_____ with an - thems sweet_____ While shep - herds watch_____ are
kings_____ sal - va - tion brings,_____ Let lov - ing hearts_____ en -

WHEN CHRIST WAS BORN OF MARY FREE

16th Century English

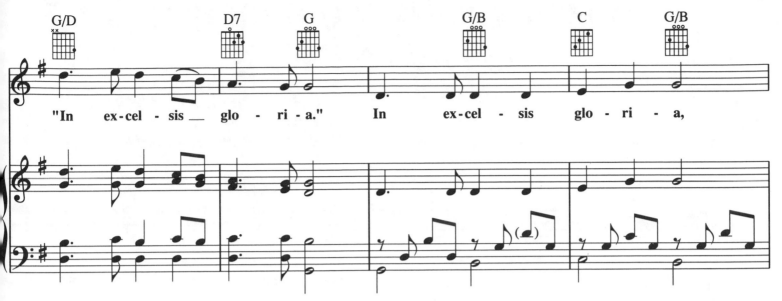

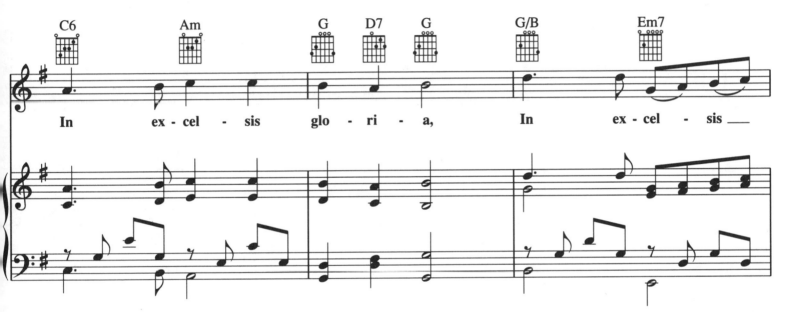

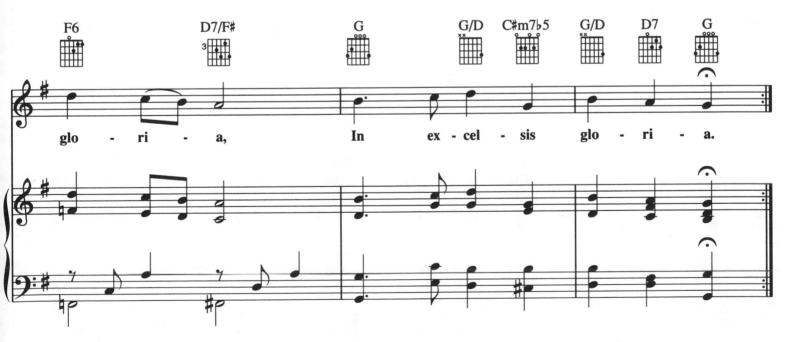

3. Then, dearest Lord, for Thy great grace,
   Grant us in bliss to see Thy Face,
   That we may to Thy solace,
   "In excelsis gloria."
   Refrain

WHEN CHRISTMAS MORN
IS DAWNING

Swedish

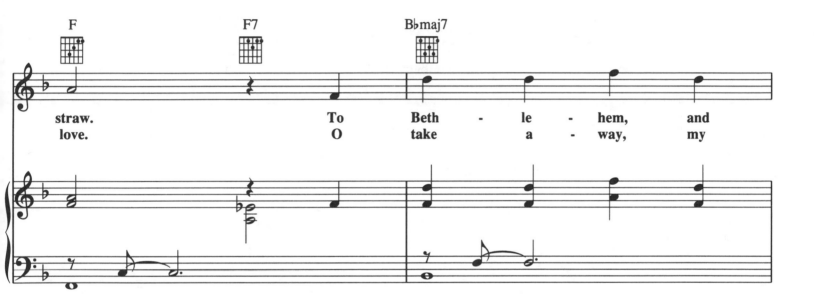

3. Blest Jesus, how I need Thee,
The children's dearest friend!
O may I never grieve Thee
With pain of sin again.

WHILE SHEPHERDS WATCHED THEIR FLOCKS BY NIGHT

Words by NAHUM TATE
Music by GEORGE F. HANDEL